BEST NEWSPAPER WRITING 1983

Modern Media Institute also publishes:

Best Newspaper Writing 1982
Best Newspaper Writing 1981
Best Newspaper Writing 1980
Best Newspaper Writing 1979
The Adversary Press
Making Sense of the News

BEST NEWSPAPER WRITING 1983

WINNERS

THE AMERICAN
SOCIETY OF
NEWSPAPER
EDITORS
COMPETITION

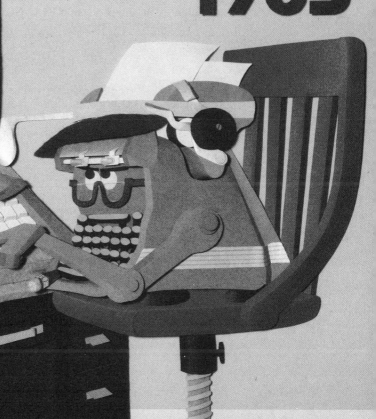

Library of Congress Cataloging in Publication Data

Best Newspaper Writing, 1979 -
    St. Petersburg, Fla., Modern Media Institute Annual
"Winners, the American Society of Newspaper
Editors' competition," Editor: 1979 - , Roy Peter Clark

Key Title: Best Newspaper Writing, ISSN 0195-895X

1. Journalism—Competitions. I. Clark, Roy Peter. II. Modern
Media Institute. III. American Society of Newspaper Editors.

PN4726.B38   081   80-646604
ISBN 0-935742-08-5

To the memory of James E. Murphy,
writer, teacher, scholar

About this book

AUGUST, 1983

If newspapers are the first rough draft of history, as an editor has said, then this book is devoted to the premise that such instant histories can be marked by literary grace as well as factual reliability.

This is Volume V of *Best Newspaper Writing,* which increasingly since 1979 has been bought by students, teachers and professionals as an indispensable text on clear, effective and graceful use of the language.

As in past years, *Best Newspaper Writing 1983* is a joint venture of the American Society of Newspaper Editors, the Modern Media Institute of St. Petersburg, Florida, and Dr. Roy Peter Clark, MMI's associate director and editor of this series of books.

Five years ago, the ASNE made better newspaper writing one of its principal long-range goals. The following year it inaugurated a contest to select the best writing in several categories from papers in the U.S. and Canada and to reward the writers with $1,000 prizes. MMI volunteered to spread the gospel of good writing by publishing the winning entries along with Clark's notes, commentaries and interviews with the winning writers. That was *Best Newspaper Writing 1979,* which is now sold out and becoming a collector's item.

Each year the winners are chosen by a panel of ASNE editors which meets in St. Petersburg for several days to screen more than 550 entries in four categories. The 1983 categories were deadline and non-deadline writing, commentary and business writing. (The judges declined to give an award this year in the deadline writing category.)

Fifteen editors, under the chairmanship of David Laventhol, publisher of *Newsday* on Long Island, made up this 1983 contest panel:

Robert L. Bartley, *Wall Street Journal*

Judith W. Brown, *New Britain* (Conn.) *Herald*

Robert W. Chandler, *Bend* (Ore.) *Bulletin*

Michael J. Davies, *Kansas City Star and Times*

Mary Anne Dolan, *Los Angeles Herald Examiner*

Katherine Fanning, *Anchorage Daily News*

Albert E. Fitzpatrick, *Akron* (Ohio) *Beacon Journal*

James B. King, *Seattle Times*

David Lawrence Jr., *Detroit Free Press*

Maxwell McCrohon, Chicago Tribune Company

Dan A. Martin, *Battle Creek* (Mich.) *Enquirer and News*

Joe Murray, *Lufkin* (Texas) *News*

Arnold Rosenfeld, *Dayton* (Ohio) *News*

James D. Squires, *Chicago Tribune*

Dr. Clark was one of the first newspaper writing coaches and has been a national leader in the growing movement to make American newspapers more readable and more interesting. Trained as a Chaucer scholar at the State University of New York, he came to the *St. Petersburg Times* in 1977 on leave from the English faculty at Auburn University for what was supposed to be a one-year sabbatical as a newsroom writing coach. The one year turned into two, the coach turned into a staff writer and then he joined MMI to direct its Writing Center. At MMI he conducts frequent writing seminars for newspaper professionals and for advanced liberal arts students seeking careers in journalism. He also works with high school students, including many minority students, college journalism teachers, high school newspaper advisors and their student editors. At a time when many despair that "kids just can't write anymore," he has developed a pilot program for fourth and fifth graders which has had remarkable success in teaching elementary school children not only to write well—but to love writing.

Clark's center is one of four at MMI which instruct students, teachers and professionals in writing, graphics, management and ethics.

Founded in 1975 by the late Nelson Poynter, chairman of the *St. Petersburg Times* and its Washington affiliate, *Congressional Quarterly,* the Modern Media Institute was bequeathed controlling stock in the Times Publishing Co. in 1978. It invests its dividends in projects such as this book, its four teaching centers and other educational and research projects, all of which seek the same goal: excellence in journalism.

Robert J. Haiman, President
Modern Media Institute

Acknowledgments

Greensboro Daily News & Record and Greta Tilley
Memphis Commercial Appeal and Rheta Grimsley Johnson
Shreveport Times and Orland Dodson
The Wall Street Journal and Manuela Hoelterhoff
The Christian Science Monitor and Rushworth Kidder
Washington Journalism Review

Portraits by Jack Barrett
Book Design by Billie M. Keirstead
Cover Sculpture by Dee Deloy

The cover for Best Newspaper Writing 1983 was
constructed entirely of paper and felt by artist
Dee Deloy of Newstart Art, Orlando, Florida.
Each piece—from the smallest key on the video
terminal to the realistic wall socket—was cut,
folded and glued into position.

Contents

Introduction

MAY, 1983

This collection begins with a story on Southern front porches and ends with an essay on New England doors.

In between you will find an interesting range of stories written by some of the best talent in American journalism. You will find features, profiles, travel, criticism, essays and columns; stories about a nun, a teen-age suicide, a murder trial, a school for girls, a German art festival, a train ride, a small Southern town, a trip through Prague; columns on high interest rates, the recession and mysterious economic numbers. You will even find an interview with economist Adam Smith, no mean discovery since the father of the "dismal science" died in 1790.

These stories were written by three winners and two finalists in the Distinguished Writing Awards competition, now in its fifth year, sponsored by the American Society of Newspaper Editors.

The winner in non-deadline writing is Greta Tilley of the *Greensboro Daily News & Record*. In business writing (a new category) the winner is Orland Dodson of the *Shreveport Times*. In commentary the winner is Rheta Grimsley Johnson, who works in the Jackson, Mississippi, bureau of the *Memphis Commercial Appeal*.

These writers lend this book a distinctively Southern flavor, one which should remind us that some of the finest literature and journalism in America has come out of the South.

The finalists are Manuela Hoelterhoff of the *Wall Street Journal* and Rushworth Kidder of the *Christian Science Monitor*, both in commentary.

This collection captures some of the best writing and reporting in America, and it should not surprise us that such excellent work comes from a bureau reporter in Mississippi as well as the arts editor of the *Wall Street Journal.*

The reader will find here vitality, compassion, humor, erudition and toughness.

Missing, however, is news.

The feature writer, the columnist, the critic, the essayist must be as timely and relevant as any reporter, for they have the chance to explore and explain the news.

But this collection contains no traditional news stories written under deadline.

ASNE gave no awards this year in the deadline writing category. David Laventhol, publisher of *Newsday* and chairman of the ASNE writing awards committee, explains: "The small number of entries submitted was perhaps not fully representative of the best deadline writing in 1982." The deadline category attracted only 54 entries out of the 557 received overall.

"At the same time," Laventhol continues, "the decision emphasizes that all of us in the newspaper business need to pay more attention to the quality of deadline writing."

What's wrong with deadline writing in American newspapers? Here are four theses: 1) Newspapers still encase even the most vivid and interesting stories in the tomb of inverted pyramids and other conventions which—in the words of the *Boston Globe*'s Alan Richman—confuse writing with outlining. 2) Editors have shifted their best talent and resources to types of writing other than deadline news. 3) Editors undervalue the best news writing in their papers, especially when it comes to writing contests. 4) We all suffer from too narrow a view of "good writing."

If I had two votes, they would be for three and four.

I read excellent deadline writing every day, in newspapers large and small.

It may describe the sentencing of Claus von Bulow; the crash of Flight 90 into the Potomac;

the basketball victory of North Carolina State;
or the election of Chicago's first black mayor.

Good writing also appears on surprising oc-
casions: a confusing day in the legislature explained; a new educational program explored; a
utility rate increase investigated.

At its best, this writing defines the news. It
is clear, interesting, concise and, on occasion,
graceful.

Perhaps during the last five years the ASNE
Distinguished Writing Awards and *Best
Newspaper Writing* have given unbalanced attention to stories that are long and unconventional.
Rarely submitted is the good, short police story,
written clearly, dramatically and responsibly; the
incisive film review written in 90 minutes on the
day the movie comes to town; or the editorial
researched and written in a single, long, arduous
day.

The best stories in American newspapers are
done quickly and under pressure. Editors need
to identify the writers and find ways to reward
them.

Good writing is not smoke and mirrors, long
leads and mixed metaphors. Good writing is
honest, clear and true to the news.

None of this should denigrate the five fine
writers whose work is celebrated here. They have
earned the attention this book will give them.

Their stories will endure the scrutiny of
thousands of reporters, editors, teachers and
students. Some will love them, some will find in
them interesting flaws, and some may not like
them at all.

In a way, that is what *Best Newspaper
Writing* is about. Despite the hyperbole of the title, this series is more about writers who aspire
to excellence than about titans of American
journalism.

This year we have asked each writer to produce a brief narrative description of how one
story was conceived and executed.

These narratives describe writers at work.

They offer techniques, feelings and second thoughts. Together, they define the sensibilities, frustrations and triumphs of most newspaper writers.

This new feature was inspired by a collection published by the *Providence Journal-Bulletin* entitled *How I Wrote the Story*. The book, compiled by reporter Chip Scanlan, is now available to the public. In a single volume, it highlights the best work produced by that newspaper. It also shares with those inside and outside the paper the best techniques of the best practitioners.

It is a fine complement to *Best Newspaper Writing*, offering models of excellence from a single newspaper.

So if, in this or any year, the writing in *Best Newspaper Writing* fails to meet your ideals or expectations, the *Providence Journal-Bulletin* offers a creative alternative.

Publish your own.

Roy Peter Clark
St. Petersburg, Florida

BEST
NEWSPAPER
WRITING
1983

Greta Tilley
Non-Deadline Writing

GRETA TILLEY, 36, is a staff writer for the *Greensboro Daily News & Record.* A native of Wilmington, North Carolina, Tilley was graduated with a degree in journalism from the University of South Carolina. She joined the staff of the *Greensboro Record* in 1969 and worked as a general assignment reporter until 1976. She left the staff that year to free-lance and rejoined the newspaper in 1979. She has won a number of awards for feature writing in the state of North Carolina.

Come sit a spell

SEPTEMBER 5, 1982

I envy Marianne and Bob Gingher, my friends in Fisher Park. They have a real front porch.

It is high-ceilinged and open, with a sloping overhang supported by rounded white columns more functional than ornate, and a gray-slatted wooden floor that covers an area neither too small nor too large—intimacy with breathing room.

The natural fence of holly bushes and nandinas forms a patchwork opening to the outside while enclosing the porch in a peace of its own. When you swing back and forth at dusk, toward the sky and away, toward the world and away, or rock in a cane-backed chair, you feel and think of things too long forgotten.

I grew up in a South of front porches, and I miss it.

I miss summer nights outside after supper; one more chance to horse around with Kenny and Ronny and Ricky and Anne Suggs while our mothers shared one last visit before scrubbing us down for bed.

I miss hearing Johnny Sellars, whose mind wouldn't let him go to school with the rest of us, singing on his front porch almost every evening, being able to tell from the cadence of his voice whether he was pacing or rocking or standing still, knowing he was safe in the world he invented in his songs.

I miss the sounds of my father laughing, and the bitter smell of his Tampa Nugget clashing with the sweet petunia blossoms in the side flower bed, and Mary Browder "oo-hooing" to my mother from across the street, and my dumb little brother racing across the grass after lightning bugs in his raggedy red Mighty Mouse cape.

The Ginghers use their porch often. The only time I sit outside my front door is when I am locked out of the house and the neighbors who keep a spare key across the street aren't home.

There are reasons.

Our ranch-style house is similar to many designed 30 or 40 years ago, when neighborhoods fled to the suburbs. The front porch isn't a porch at all, but a miniscule concrete-and-brick bridge between four steps and the front door, behind which hums the central air conditioning system we installed during a heat-induced delirium last summer.

There is no way for anyone sitting on the top step to escape a clobbering when the door is opened, no space for a rocking chair, much less a swing.

There would be no need to build a bigger porch. Like most other houses on our block, ours is too far away from the street to give a proper holler to people jogging by, whom we don't know anyway, and who probably wouldn't break stride to stop.

Although front porches aren't found only in territories below the Mason-Dixon line, they surely must have been born here, for they are as characteristic of the South as you-alls and magnolia blossoms.

"It's where you smell the summer night," says Chapel Hill professor-novelist Max Steele. Which smells like "lightning bugs if you're small, and like ferns in clay pots, and canna lilies, and the grass cut that afternoon; the dusty brick smell if you had columns on your porch, the rotting wood smell if the gutter leaked. If you talked to somebody in the house, it smelled like dusty screens. Remember that smell?"

If people were sitting on their porches, it meant they were home and receiving. Stop by without coming inside and seeing my dirty dishes, the message went. Stop by and we'll see what develops.

Many important works of fiction unfolded on the Southern front porch. Tom Sawyer schemed

there. Eugene Gant in *Look Homeward, Angel*
loved there, on a porch designed after Thomas
Wolfe's own in his hometown of Asheville. Many
of Eudora Welty's *Losing Battles* were fought
there. Boo Radley finally made friends with Scout
on Atticus Finch's front porch swing in *To Kill
A Mockingbird.*

But as a New South strode eagerly toward
a new set of dreams, middle-class Southerners
sent the front porch to the back yard. They
screened or glassed it in, built a patio or a deck,
and pulled the drapes on yet another window to
their past.

Progress did much of it. Air conditioning
made it so folks didn't have to go outside to cool
off, and television evolved from a novelty picture
box to conquer our senses. The economy did some
talking, too.

And people started getting busy. They
became homogenized and specialized and prefer-
red to socialize indoors. They forgot how to make
front porch conversation, the kind that begins
nowhere and ends nowhere, but means
something just the same. Maybe they even forgot
how to listen.

"The telephone," Steele says, "has replaced
the front porch. Everything that happens to
students happens now on the telephone. They
don't know how to talk to each other in person."

Some say front porches are making a comeback. Look in the newer subdivisions, some will
tell you, at the country-style and Victorian-style
and rice-planter-style houses.

"If you go out on Jefferson Road," says
Greensboro builder Harold Odenwald, "turn
right off Friendly Avenue and go about six
blocks, you'll see two new houses right there that
have full porches across the front.

"The kind of house we grew up in, that's what
people are looking for. People are seeing how attractive houses are when they're restored, like
in the College Hill area, and they're picking up
that style and carrying them to the suburbs."

But the prospect for a real comeback is suspect. "Too much air conditioning and too much noise," says Betty Silver, head of the state Association of Architects. "Front porches now are just for show."

Furnishings on these new old-style front porches bear out Silver's analysis. Some have a swing, but no rocking chairs or lounge chairs for company. Some have only hanging baskets or potted plants.

A beautiful porch borders the front of a house in The Thicket, a subdivision off West Wendover Avenue. But instead of chairs, it is decorated with some sort of birdhouse and other knick-knacks.

On many nouveau-old porches, the only piece of furniture is a deacon's bench, and everybody knows you can't do any serious sitting on stiff-slatted boards.

In older neighborhoods where people are renovating old houses, and in working-class neighborhoods where people find strength in simplicity, the front porch isn't making a comeback because it never went anywhere in the first place.

Stroll one evening along Carr Street in the College Hill section downtown, or down Asheboro Street a few miles south, or in the Glenwood community in the southwest. People are sitting on porches.

Walk along Florida Street past Smith Homes, and you'll see some front porches that weren't there 10 years ago.

The oldest housing project in Greensboro had no porches then, only tiny stoops with rotting wood and loose railings. The housing authority sent out a survey to see what residents wanted most. The answer was decent front porches.

Clementine Jones uses hers almost every day. She punches out at 3 p.m. from her job as housekeeper in the physical plant at UNC-G, rushes home to catch "General Hospital," throws some dinner on the stove, slides into her black scuffs, and heads for the front porch.

Her friend across the way, Janie Mae Kimbell, usually joins her, because Jones' porch is positioned for a better view of the passing scene.

"I call my front porch my relaxing place," Jones says, because I get out here and just relax. My son comes by sometimes to visit and we sit out here and talk. My grandbaby, he's 2, he'll be 3 soon, he comes out here and has a ball.

"There's just something about the front porch that people like. I get out here and watch the people and cars, see what's going on. It's not that you're being nosy, but you don't have to go to a movie."

Almost any night after supper, down one of the shady, narrow roads perpendicular to Spring Garden Street, a friendly couple named Viola and Amos Wood are out on their porch.

On a summer evening, he may be wearing a sleeveless undershirt tucked into khaki work pants; she, canvas pumps and shorts. He probably will be sitting in a large woven lounge chair; she in a wrought-iron chaise lounge cushioned in flowered vinyl.

Like many of their neighbors, the Woods' front porch habit is a family tradition. They grew up in rural areas. They are retired from the hosiery mill where they first saw each other, a few blocks from the home they built 42 years ago.

When the weather cooperates, they pass the nights on their small, comfortable front porch, set close to the sidewalk and closer to a large oak tree.

"I just enjoy sitting out in the fresh air," Amos says. "If I didn't have a porch, I'd build one. See," he says, looking into the night, "there's a lady across the street there. She sees us and comes on out and sits out on her porch."

"I think she's like me," Viola interjects. "Sits to see what's going on. Oh, and some nights we sit and see the moon coming out and it's just beautiful with the stars and all.

"Hear those young boys yonder? We wouldn't hear that with the TV on. Might miss something that goes on in the apartments around here, too.

We stay out to 11 o'clock, past that. I enjoy listening to that."

Amos continues to stare ahead. "We most
always have something to talk about."

Viola agrees. "There's plenty to discuss."

"We were just talking about when I was a
kid," Amos says. "I'd go out where they were cur-
ing tobacco out around the tobacco barn, make
me a pallet and sleep in the grass under the
stars."

My friend Jane Turpin drives the 23 miles
from her home in an outer corner of Randleman
to downtown Greensboro each workday. She moved from the city to the country to taste the kinds
of things Amos Wood grew up knowing.

Jane sees the practical side of porches.
"They're good to rock on," she says. "If you try
to rock out in the yard, you run into tree roots
and rocks and depressions. They're also good to
shell peas on and stuff."

She gets ornery when people mention screen-
ing them in.

"If you do that," she says, "you might as well
pull your rocking chair up to the window. You
want the fresh air smell, the smell of chicken
manure along with the flowers.

"That's what's wrong with society.
Everything's rush-rush, and nobody's taking
time to sniff."

That's what front porches should be for. For
sniffing and slamming screen doors, for swatting
at mosquitoes and sipping iced tea from frosted-
over glasses, for painting fingernails and
braiding hair, for snapping beans while forget-
ting about cookies burning in the oven, for
reading the evening paper under the fading light
of dusk, for whispering secrets and promises that
might not be kept.

Jane Turpin is right. When people abandoned front porches to chase life, they ran past the
best part.

Observations and questions

1) Five of the first seven paragraphs begin with the word "I." Many journalists are discouraged from using the word in their work. What is the effect of using the first person in this story? What kind of story would it have been without it?

2) We all have familiar characters out of our past who sometimes find their way into our writing. What effect does the writer create by introducing us to characters such as Anne Suggs and Johnny Sellars?

3) Most of the sentences used by Tilley in this story are *cumulative*. That means that the subject and verb of the main clause come at the beginning of the sentence. Cumulative sentences tend to be clear and direct even when they are long, because the reader never has to search for the subject and verb: "*I envy* Marianne and Bob Gingher, my friends in Fisher Park'," or "*It is* high-ceilinged and open, with a sloping overhang supported by rounded white columns more functional than ornate, and a gray-slatted wooden floor that covers an area neither too small nor too large — intimacy with breathing room." Look throughout this book for sentences with a similar structure. Examine your own work to see if you are writing sentences of this type.

4) Writers use *periodic* sentences — in which the main clause comes last — for variation. Such sentences often surprise the reader with interesting effects: "When you swing back and forth at dusk, toward the sky and away, toward the world and away, or rock in a cane backed chair, you feel and think of things too long forgotten." In a way, the form of this sentence reflects

its meaning, as if it were a poem. The sentence swings back and forth before reaching the main clause. Examine how the writer accomplishes this.

5) Good writers appeal to all the senses to help a reader vicariously experience a scene or event. Read this story again and examine the passages which appeal to sight, sound, taste, touch and smell.

6) The writer, herself a Southerner, uses dialect, such as *ornery* and *yonder*. Is this appropriate to the subject of the story or does it distract the reader? Sometimes dialect can be used unfairly, to stereotype or ridicule a person. Southerners often find themselves the victims of such language prejudice. Examine the way in which Tilley characterizes the speech of Clementine Jones. Does she handle this in a sensitive and responsible manner?

7) Would this story be better if it ended a paragraph sooner?

The dean of discipline is an angel of mercy

APRIL 18, 1982

If the situation calls for it, Sister Genevieve can come out with a pretty impressive scowl. Just ask her about the beans.

There they were, 1,000 cans—she counted every one of them—stacked against the convent wall. Not green beans. The nourishing kind. Pork and beans.

So Sister went on another tear. No more beans, she announced to the dark-stained rafters of St. Mary's Catholic Church. The poor do not need pork and beans. They need greens, salmon, peanut butter, corn, fruit, grits. They need nourishment.

Soon, signs began appearing on the wall above Sister's seat in the rear of the sanctuary, specifying food needs for the month. Sister selects the menu.

As parishioners pass through the vestibule toward Sunday Mass, they face a photograph of Sister Genevieve, her smile as bright as a votive candle, her arms cradling a 10-pound can of pork and beans. Below is a box for donations.

Sister runs most of her business this way. Official church documents title her "pastoral associate," but that's not what people call her. They call her Dean of Discipline.

Each Sunday she reigns from a wooden schoolhouse chair, welcoming parishioners to the church on Duke Street, taking children to the bathroom, moving them next to her if they misbehave. Sometimes she cues the organist.

She coordinates youth education and heads the liturgy committee.

And tends the poor.

Her neighbors and many parishioners are black; her bosses, Catholic. But religion and race don't matter. Sister Genevieve helps anybody she believes worthy.

From her simply furnished home base in southeast Greensboro, she moves about town, praying at high Masses and wakes, climbing ladders and stocking larders, delivering demands to politicians and support to prisoners, whose company she likes best.

She brings along the twinkle of a child, the roar of a lion, a running discourse with the Lord, and a laugh that turns on the lights.

She is a con artist in the purest sense, dealing and wheeling, dreaming and scheming, fast-talking and swapping. She stops at robbing the rich to give to the poor. She doesn't need to. She could coax the key to the vault from Ebenezer Scrooge.

A woman from Ohio had been sending her clothes for years. "I kept thinking," Sister says, "if you can send me these clothes, you can send me some money."

The woman now sends checks.

Her philosophy is "always accept."

"Like Thanksgiving," Genevieve says. "A man asked, 'Sister, have you got a project?' 'Oh yeah, oh yeah,' I answered. Never say no. If I don't have one, I come home and think of one."

She called back and asked for 26 chickens and trimmings. Thanksgiving dinner for the poor.

Some people compare Sister Genevieve to Mother Teresa, the Nobel Prize-winning nun. Like Teresa, she believes there can be no social legislation to help the poor. "We must do it ourselves," Sister says, "with love. All that time we spend griping about budget cuts and depending on someone else could be used creatively to do things on our own. If each person could take care of just one or two people a week."

"The problem with humans," Genevieve says, waving her hands, "is that they want to do great things. Big things. We don't want to do piddling things. Well, the things we do are these little piddly things no one else wants to do, and we come out on top, anyway. Isn't that right, Lord?"

* * *

Genevieve Noonan was prepped for life by a Catholic school in Richmond, Va., and a mother who at some time or other cooked for most people in the neighborhood where they lived.

Her future unfolded one fall afternoon when she tagged along with Sister Romana Walsh to visit the poor. "We walked up a long fire escape of this old building," Genevieve says. "I can see the woman's expression now. She opened the door and there was such agony on her face. But when she saw Sister she said, 'Come children, our angel is here.' Her whole expression changed. I was 9 years old but I never forgot it. I went home and told my mother I wanted to be an angel. I dated, danced, did all the things I wanted to in high school, but I never got the image out of my mind. I had to be that angel to others. That had to be my life."

When she completed her spiritual training, Genevieve was told to keep her own name. For Saint Genevieve, patroness of Paris. During the French Revolution, Saint Genevieve kept things calm.

Sister Genevieve is calm only when she sleeps or prays. She doesn't sleep that much, but she prays often. "That's my asset," she says.

When children misbehave in Sunday School, she says, "Let us pray," and sometimes teaches a 10-minute lesson to bowed heads. "If anybody really bothers you, just start praying with them," Sister says. "You've got 'em. They can't move."

Genevieve Noonan stormed into the Daughters of Charity of St. Vincent de Paul in Emmitsburg, Md., a 117-pound nun in a 10-pound habit, ready to butt heads with the injustices of the world. She has no patience with injustice. "I would've killed him," she says after hearing about a man who beat his wife. She once chased down a longshoreman in a Baltimore alley, then demanded to know why he beat his child.

The years—she won't say how many—have
added a few pounds and shortened her skirts, but
not relieved her of the uniform. "I fight for this
habit," she says. "We could not get into places
without them, like jail. People respect you.
They're afraid God's going to smite them down
or something if they aren't nice to us. They give
us preferential treatment."

She has worked along the East Coast from
New York to Florida, in jails, in mental institu-
tions, in homes for deserted and handicapped
children. "I used to pray that I would come to
the black community," she says. "It took me 30
years to get here."

* * *

Nine years ago, Sister Genevieve moved into the convent house at 1212 Gorrell St. and
started working her little miracles.

The St. Mary's social ministry fund has no
budget. Money comes from donations, which
come in with little predictability. But they come.

So do emergencies. So Sister begs. From
Father Daniel Kramer. From the 200
parishioners. From strangers. From the Lord.

Sister doesn't worry much. As a child, she
made a deal with Martin de Porres, her favorite
saint. She says devotionals to him, he watches
over her. Saint Martin carries the heavier end
of the bargain.

"When I came here I had a brand new $1 bill
somebody gave me," she says. "I said, 'Saint Martin, you know I have to have $1,000 to take care
of all these people.' Well, he's got me $1,200 since
I've been in this house here, not counting the
clothes and food and refrigerators and all, so he's
doing very well."

Other nuns, all white, have lived in the
convent before Genevieve. Her order has no black
sisters in its southeastern province. Fifty years
ago, St. Mary's first nuns needed an OK from
City Hall. A law forbade whites from living in
black neighborhoods.

The congregation, once all-black, now has
almost as many whites. When economics closed

the parochial school in the mid-'70s, four nuns were sent off to other communities.

Genevieve's housemate moved out because of illness, and for a hectic five months, she worked alone. Then Sister Irene moved in.

These two nuns who call themselves "The Odd Couple" and carry an "I Love New York" sticker on the back bumper of the parish Citation, radiate enough electricity to reach Vatican City.

They love the neighborhood and their neighbors, and crusade for both.

"I go to a City Council meeting and they smile at me," Sister Genevieve says. "I don't want them to smile, I want them to listen. I always sit in the front row."

"You see her tracks all over town," says fuel company owner Joe Berry, target for many of Sister's appeals. "She's quite a woman."

When the sisters encounter prejudice, such as the man in the pickup truck who yelled at them one evening to "watch out for niggers," Genevieve turns once again to Martin, her dark-skinned saint.

She writes the offender's name, if she knows it, on a tiny square of paper and puts it underneath de Porres' statue on the table by her front door. It stays there until Sister decides penance has been done.

"I've always wanted to be like Joan of Arc, to lead an army or something," Genevieve says. "I've never gotten to do that.

"Well, I guess I lead my own little armies."

* * *

It is another typically untypical day.

Sister Genevieve rises at six and meets Irene in the upstairs chapel for prayer. Together, they join the three priests in the parish house next door for Mass. After a simple breakfast of coffee, fruit and toast, and a spiritual reading and discussion, the sisters part ways.

Genevieve sorts clothes for the emergency clothing store across from the convent, scowling at the pieces with holes. The poor have pride.

She collects food from the cardboard box in the church vestibule and trots the bagful of cans to the convent basement, showing no respect for the steep steps.

She gives away a refrigerator and mattress and begins checking credentials of candidates for Guilford County sheriff. She wants a new one. "More cooperation at the jail."

Sisters Genevieve and Irene then climb into a four-wheel drive truck for a trip to Swenson's, where a friend is treating them to lunch.

The first thing Sister Genevieve does after sliding into the booth is pocket a few packets of sugar. After chick-filet and burger specials, they eat ice cream, small spoonfuls at a time, and chat with a young waitress who tells them she has never seen real live nuns before. "Do they really make you scrub floors?"

Irene talks about life with Genevieve. Shortly after moving to Greensboro, she found what it would be like. The two sisters had traveled to a diocesan conference in Charlotte, where they shared a room.

"Early the next morning, I was awakened by this thud." Irene says, "and felt something wet all over my face. Genevieve was running in place by the bed, splashing Holy Water all over me."

Her legs still churning, Sister Genevieve called to Irene, "Live Jesus." The proper Catholic response is "Forever in our hearts," but Irene didn't answer that way. "I opened one eye," Irene says, "and said, 'I hate you.' "

Sister Irene becomes serious.

"Genevieve has things very much in perspective in her own life," she says, "and this crystallizes for other people. There is no other like her."

As Irene praises, Genevieve begins to cry.

"We can't keep enough Kleenex," Irene says. "I always stock up at the grocery store."

* * *

Georgia McTier lives in southeast Greensboro. She's arthritic, blind and decisive.

Visitors must call her "Aunt Georgia." On her 106th birthday in June, she wants Sister Genevieve to arrange a high Mass in her living room on South Booker Street.

It is Monday afternoon, and Sister has come to assure Aunt Georgia her house will wear a new coat of paint by Sunday.

A few weeks before, a city inspector had knocked at Aunt Georgia's front door. The house must be painted, he said, or a condemned sign would be posted.

Aunt Georgia called Sister Genevieve. Sister Genevieve called Father Kramer. Father Kramer said to find some paint. So Genevieve begged 18 cans from a man she didn't know.

It was settled. Sister, Father Kramer and some helpers would climb the ladder to scrape, then paint.

"No sign," Sister has come to tell Aunt Georgia. No condemned sign on the front lawn. The women are clasping hands on the couch, snuggled about as close as two people can be.

"I wanted to be a Sister so bad," Aunt Georgia says. "I wanted to wear me some beads around my waist and a big wide bonnet. But my daddy said no, there were too many of us, and he couldn't see his way to let me be a Sister. Oh, how I used to sit and weep about it."

Sister Genevieve nods. She has heard the story before.

"My sister in Philadelphia thinks she made heaven and earth," Aunt Georgia says, hugging Genevieve. "I believe she did but won't tell us.

"God just dropped her out of heaven. We needed somebody so bad, so he brought us our angel."

As the two rock back and forth, Aunt Georgia rubs her hand over Sister Genevieve's skirt. "Getting the good off," she says. "I rub it off and put it on me."

Too bad Sister Irene isn't around. Genevieve could use some Kleenex.

Observations and questions

1) The writer chooses to begin the story of Sister Genevieve with a scene. Does this scene provide an adequate focus for the story? If not, can you find an element that might have worked more effectively?

2) This story has an almost circular structure. We discover at the beginning that this woman became a nun because she saw what it meant to become an angel of mercy to another human being. At the end of the story, we witness her become that angel. Do you think the writer chose wisely in taking advantage of that structure? Does it seem too pat?

3) This is the story of a white Catholic nun who ministers to a black neighborhood in an essentially Protestant city. Do you think the writer emphasizes these circumstances sufficiently?

4) The writer refrains from cynicism or skepticism concerning the nun's way of life. She accepts the nun's faith on its own terms, offers it to the reader and lets the reader deal with it. Could the writer have done this if the subject were not a "Mother Teresa" type, but a Scientologist or a member of the Unification Church?

5) Were you surprised by the quote, "I would've killed him"? What does that reveal about the character of Sister Genevieve?

6) Consider the way in which the writer uses language and imagery that seem appropriate to a story about a Catholic nun: "her smile as bright as a votive candle"; "These two nuns...radiate enough electricity to reach Vatican City"; "She

brings along the twinkle of a child, the roar of
a lion, a running discourse with the Lord, and
a laugh that turns on the lights."

7) St. Martin de Porres is the sister's patron
saint. We don't find out much about him in this
story. Consult the *New Catholic Encyclopedia* to
find out more about the life and legend of the
saint. Would you have used any of this information in the story?

8) Tilley uses a number of intentional sentence
fragments in her work. Some readers find these
distracting, even when they come from a skilled
writer. Read them over. Write them into complete sentences. Decide which style is more
effective.

9) The writer senses a tension between the
nun's spirituality and practicality, between her
desire to be Joan of Arc and her need to collect
cans of food. Explore how the writer deals with
these two sides of Sister's personality.

A suicide at age 16

FEBRUARY 7, 1982

Seven weeks have passed, yet the dim lavender room with the striped window curtains has been kept as Tonja left it.

Haphazardly positioned on top of the white French provincial-style dresser are staples of teen-age life: Sure deodorant, Enjoli cologne, an electric curling wand.

A white jewelry box opens to a ballerina dancing before a mirror. Inside, among watches and bracelets, is a gold Dudley High School ring with a softball player etched into one side and a Panther on the other. Also inside is a mimeographed reminder that a $9 balance must be paid in Mrs. Johnson's room for the 1982 yearbook. The deadline was Jan. 15.

Next to a junior high honor society certificate is a plaque inscribed to the winner of the first Terry McClured Citizenship Award, given in memory of the late Gillespie Junior High School principal who died two years ago after a courageous fight against Hodgkin's disease. Tonja was in the ninth grade when she was chosen by her teachers to receive it.

Signs of life have not left the room. On the bureau, next to neatly folded socks and underwear, rests the small stuffed panda Tonja slept with since her mother gave it to her nine years ago.

In a place always reserved on the right-hand corner of the dresser, a navy and white Panther baseball cap lies over a baseball glove, its once-taut leather softened by hundreds of catches at third base.

Brightly painted figures of children wearing baggy overalls, skillfully drawn on poster paper, hang on opposite walls. They have compelling captions and solemn faces. "Love Me," says an orange-haired boy crying large blue tears. "I'm Lonely."

Basically, the room is the same—with one grim exception. When Tonja left it for the last time six days before Christmas, a .22-caliber rifle lay jammed between the mattress and right bedpost at the foot of the canopied bed.

On this cold January morning, the bed is covered with school homework papers, letters, a directory of colleges, a family photo album and high school and junior high yearbooks, which Douglas Oxendine eagerly has taken from his daughter's closet and drawers to help open her life to a stranger.

Near the spot where the rifle once was lodged is a large cardboard box. Inside are nine manila envelopes, each tagged with a Greensboro Police Department label.

In the hours after Tonja's death, Detective Ken Brady was particularly interested in the single sheet of notebook paper marked "Evidence No. 12." In uneven, penciled script, lines of poetry are listed along with corresponding page numbers that show where the poems can be found in the 11th-grade literature book, *Encounters.* Each poem is about death.

Also among Tonja's papers is a newspaper article about the rise in teen-age suicides:

"In many cases, psychiatrists claim the tendencies of troubled young people to self-destruct are overlooked until it is too late, because their aberrant behavior is chalked up to growing pains or is simply ignored."

Messages from teachers and friends crowd the slick pages of four yearbooks. For Tonja, life was full of promise.

"You are sweet, nice, crazy, smart"... "sometimes I thought we would never stop laughing"... "you are like a daughter and I love you as one"... "you are a ray of sunshine in my class"... "like a sister to me"... "I don't know what I'd do without you. Keep your chin up and a smile on your face and life will take you far."

And this:

"It has really been nice knowing you and being on the softball team with you. You are a very
intelligent, bright young lady. From now to your
death you will have my friendship to call your
own....

"Your friend Vikky Falls."

In high school yearbooks and to teen-agers
like Vikky Falls, life stretches ahead forever. For
Tonja Faye Oxendine, it lasted 16 years and
three months.

* * *

As a homicide detective with the Greensboro
Police Department, Brady has investigated
dozens of suicides. "Ten, 15, 20 years ago, you
rarely heard of young people killing themselves,"
he says, "The typical suicide victim was a white
male in his 50s. That wouldn't be the case today.
It would be teen-agers and young adults."

To those like Brady who did not know her,
Tonja's death becomes another sad statistic.

But to her father, brother, friends and
teachers, it has brought misery and unanswered
questions. They ponder the last time they saw
her, the conversations, looking for clues, realiz-
ing too late what might have been a signal, lay-
ing blame—often too harshly—on themselves.

This is the way of suicides. In Tonja Oxendine's case it is more pronounced because the
evidence is not as clear. There were no obvious
warnings, no long periods of depression.

No boyfriend was involved. Tonja rarely
dated. The last time she seemed troubled over
a boy was the previous February, when she and
a friend, Sue Ann Canady, fell for the same guy
at Holiday Roller Rink.

Tonja was not without material possessions.
Oxendine, a line mechanic for E. R. Squibb &
Son, operates on a tight budget but managed to
provide the extension telephone, stereo-tape
player and portable television set in her bedroom.

"The one thing she wanted more than
anything else was a car," says Marilyn Mitchell,

Tonja's aunt, who lives next door. "We told her
we'd try to help her get one in February. She said
she was counting on that."

Like most teen-agers, Tonja sometimes had
disagreements with her father, particularly when
she wanted to go out with girlfriends two or three
years older whom she had met through athletics.
And the night before she died, Tonja and her
father had what seemed like a typical father-
daughter disagreement.

But family and close friends say that Tonja
cared deeply for her father and brother.

There were also mood swings, but they seemed nothing beyond common teen-age behavior.

"Two or three months ago Tonja had gone
through this stage of acting different," says Mitchell. "She stopped coming around and seemed
withdrawn. It really hurt me because we were
so close, but I thought it was something that
would pass over. My teen-age boys went through
the same thing.

"The last three or four weeks before she died,
she went through a complete turnaround. She
was so happy and full of life, just like the old
Tonja."

Tammy Dickerson, a friend who saw Tonja
the night before she died, said she was the happiest person she had ever seen.

This is a pattern with suicide victims, says
Brady. They appear content, even elated, before
the end. "It's almost a relief. They have made
their decision and don't have to debate it any
more. Few suicides are impulsive."

* * *

Why would a talented, well-liked teen-ager
take a 40-inch rifle, position the muzzle against
the right side of her abdomen and reach over and
squeeze the trigger? How could such unresolved
pain live inside a girl with a smile like Tonja's?

There are theories, but no one can be sure.
Tonja did not leave a note.

Those close to her are positive of one thing.
She didn't mean to die. She was asking for help.

Although Tonja's death certificate reads suicide, Brady agrees it could have been accidental. "Most people who intend to actually kill themselves with a gun hold it to their head or between their eyes," he says. "Few shoot themselves in the side."

Like most suicide cases, this one has complexities and contradictions.

Tonja Oxendine was caring and generous, sensitive and hardworking. She liked sports so much she once became the only girl on the Elks Club softball team, where she learned to field barbs as adeptly as pop flies. She collected rocks and Steve Garvey clippings. She was dependable and good with children.

"She had this ability to love people no matter who they were or what they did," says April Kiser, a close friend who lives down the street. "She cared about everybody and never was hateful, even when they were hateful to her."

When Ted and April Craddock became parents of a 4-pound baby with a mild case of cerebral palsy, they had trouble finding baby sitters. "People were scared to handle him since he was so small," April Craddock says. "But the first time Tonja laid eyes on him, she just took him over. She treated him just like we wanted people to treat him, as a normal child. She took him with her everywhere. And when we came for him, he didn't want to leave his Tonja."

Most of all, there was her smile.

"It wasn't a phony smile and it wasn't a distressed smile," says Mitchell. "It was always there. To find something behind that smile you'd have to go very, very deep, deeper I think, than Tonja wanted anybody to go."

Descriptions of Tonja's personality and manner don't always match. Some saw her as outgoing, some as friendly but quiet, others as a combination of both. At times she could be like two different people, enthusiastic one minute, morose the next. Only those closest to her, however, saw the somber side.

"She was so mixed up about life and people," says Tammy Dickerson. "Why people were like they were and why they said one thing and did another, why people she cared about didn't always care about her. She looked for the good in everybody and if they weren't as good as she thought, she went into deep depressions."

All who knew Tonja say she was constantly searching for reassurance and approval. She seemed almost obsessively driven to make new friends, then to constantly test the friendships. She became easily hurt if, in her analysis, the test failed.

"She was always apologizing to me for everything when she hadn't done anything," Dickerson says. "Even when she opened up, I felt she really wasn't telling everything. It seemed like she wanted to, but she just couldn't."

Instead, Tonja did much of her emotional juggling alone.

"When somebody has a problem I try to help them the best I can," Tonja wrote last year in a letter to Sue Ann Canady, "but when I have a problem, no one cares about mine or tries to help me. So I feel left out, which I am."

"Tonja was always saying something was wrong; then, when you asked her what it was, she'd say 'nothing,' " says Karen Nance, a Smith High School sophomore Tonja visited the night before she died.

"She was so well-liked and respected," says Mary Jo Lentz, Tonja's coach at Dudley. "The sad part is she didn't realize how much."

* * *

Tonja Faye Oxendine was born in Southeastern General Hospital in Lumberton. Her father, a Lumbee Indian from McDonald, a small community in Robeson County, and her mother, Shirley, a native of Michigan, had been married a year and a day.

By the time Tonja turned 7, Oxendine had moved his family five times, usually looking for better-paying jobs. He finally settled in a rural area of Lincoln County, five miles from Lincolnton.

It was there, Oxendine says, that the family, which then included 5-year-old Chris, was the happiest. It was also there, when Tonja was 8 years old, that another gunshot shattered their lives.

On April 27, 1973, Shirley Oxendine, pregnant with a third child, was shot in the chest as she slept on the sofa at home. At the preliminary hearing in a Lincoln County court, the judge found no evidence to try Douglas Oxendine on charges of involuntary manslaughter.

"Her hobby was skeet-shooting," says Oxendine. "She was lying on the couch and I was cleaning her gun. She had dropped it in the mud the day before. The phone rang and I went to answer it. When I came back I picked it up and started oiling it.

"It went off. Shirley sat straight up and said, 'What's that?' At first I thought it hit Chris but I saw he wasn't hurt and I was relieved. Then I saw Shirley holding her chest. I thought I had unloaded all the shells."

Tonja had been at school. When Oxendine told her later, he says, a strange look crossed her face, but she showed little emotion. "Daddy," she said, "can I go out to play?"

Oxendine resisted his mother's pleas to move home to Robeson County. He was determined to rear the children on his own. When Lincolnton became too painful, he moved to a small, green-shingled home off Freeman Mill Road in Greensboro, next door to his sister, and decorated it with green plants and family photographs.

"I know Tonja missed having a mother, but I tried to compensate as much as I could," says Mitchell. "She was like a daughter."

"We tried to keep her mother's memory alive, but Tonja refused to talk about her, even to me. She wouldn't go back to Lincolnton. Last April, her father wanted her to go with him to put some flowers on Shirley's grave, but she absolutely refused to go."

Meanwhile, Tonja's life in Greensboro seemed to flourish. Teachers at Gillespie Junior High School say she touched many lives.

"She was one of the few kids I really remember, attitude-wise, who was a perfect all-round student," says Mary Setzer, who taught Tonja in several classes.

"Tonja was a rarity, an athlete with brains," says Coach Deborah Jones. "She was an inspiration and a challenge."

School life at Dudley was different. Teachers knew her as a student who attended class regularly and did her work.

But she was reserved, neither a standout nor a troublemaker. She rarely spoke unless spoken to and seldom asked questions. While her grades were good enough to make honor roll and honor society at Gillespie, they were average or slightly above at Dudley.

Where Tonja did excel was on the athletic field. She lettered in softball her sophomore year and even collected a few votes for all-conference. Coach Lentz told Tonja that, barring injuries, she had a good shot at making the all-conference team this year.

Tonja went out for volleyball last fall and, although she wasn't a starter, became a specialist who came into the game to serve. She was delighted when her name appeared in the newspaper for serving 15 points in a row.

Lentz is convinced Tonja could have won a college athletic scholarship. She also believes she could have helped if Tonja had told her something was wrong. "Tonja came into my office the week before she died," Lentz says. "She asked if she could start working out in the gym after Christmas to get ready for softball season. She seemed so excited."

Much of Tonja's life revolved around personal relationships. She spent hours each day talking on the telephone and writing letters to friends.

Many of these notes reflected insecurity. While some can be attributed to teen-age paranoia, it goes deeper.

"Maybe I don't belong out there or maybe I don't belong to anyone," she told Sue Ann in a note about the roller skating rink. "I was thinking about selling my skates, anyway.

"Maybe he doesn't like me because I am a different race. I am not good enough for him or anyone else, I guess. I am just out of place (at the skating rink)."

Yet friends say Tonja seemed proud of her Indian heritage, speaking of it often and occasionally helping at the Guilford Native American Center, which two weeks ago held a memorial in her honor.

In a letter to Tammy Dickerson: "See, I have a lot of things on my mind and I don't say anything about it. I'm not used to being open with anyone because I've never had anyone I could really talk to."

* * *

The next-to-last day of Tonja's life was a full one.

After homeroom, she went to Spanish I, where the teacher, Sheila Clendenning, passed out progress reports for the nine-week period. Tonja's grade had dropped from a C-plus to a D, but she had until Jan. 19 to pull it up.

Two things happened that were uncharacteristic of Tonja. She was caught writing a note in class, something Clendenning hadn't seen her do before.

"I didn't make a scene or anything, I just leaned over and asked her to put it away," Clendenning says. "I wonder now if I should have taken it."

The Monday before, Tonja hadn't done her homework. It was the only time in nine weeks she didn't turn in an assignment.

In Laura Hooks' fifth-period Literature II class, Tonja was one of the students called on to recite a poem from memory. She walked to the front of the room and repeated, flawlessly, Sonnet No. 106 by William Shakespeare.

The following Monday, the class would be tested on figurative language. Since they started the study on poetry Dec. 8, students had been reading poems and picking out examples of similes, metaphors, personification and hyperbole.

In one section, many of the poems dealt with death. For homework, the class had been assigned to find similes and metaphors. Hooks believes the piece of notebook paper police found in Tonja's *Encounters* book had something to do with that homework. But she also assigned poems that aren't about dying. Tonja may have listed them on another sheet of paper, but they weren't found among her things.

Early that Friday evening, Tonja walked next door to her Aunt Marilyn's. She told her she was going to the Northeast High School-Western Guilford girls' basketball game and asked if the outfit she was wearing looked all right.

"She seemed real happy and excited," Mitchell says. "She had on a beige pair of cords and a beige blazer and asked if they went together. I told her no, they didn't, they were too much the same color. She said she'd never get dressed in time. I told her, 'Well, please don't wear that.' She said she wouldn't and we laughed. It was the last time I saw her."

Shortly before 6:30, Tonja picked up Tammy Dickerson at her apartment. She was driving her father's silver Grand Torino. Tonja, who had invited Tammy the Monday before, insisted on buying the $2 tickets. She had wanted to see the game because Michele Graves, a girl she met a few weeks before, played for Northeast. One of Tonja's close friends, Donna McClintock, played point guard.

After the game, Tonja stopped by the locker room to talk to Donna, who had passed her in the lobby earlier but didn't speak. Tonja wanted to see if she was mad. Donna said no, she just hadn't seen Tonja as she walked by. She said their date to go roller skating Saturday night was still on. Tonja said she would pick her up.

Tonja, Tammy and Michele then drove out to see Lisa Scarce, another friend from Northeast who lives with her grandparents. In a few hours, Tonja left to take Michele home.

Like he always does, Oxendine, who works the 2 to 11 p.m. shift, called Tonja at home between 10:30 and 11 p.m. to make sure everything was all right. "I'll see you when I get home," he told her. "Don't go off again."

But when another friend, Karen Nance, called, Tonja told her she was upset and needed to talk to her. She drove over to Karen's house behind Hunter Elementary School.

"When she got there, she started talking about the game and everything," says Karen, a 10th grade softball player from Smith High School. "She never said what was bothering her.

"She always did that. She'd tell you something was wrong and wouldn't tell you what. She would leave you hanging."

Tonja did say she thought Michele was mad at her and tried to call her from Karen's house but couldn't reach her. When she left, she started crying. "What's wrong?" Karen asked. "Nothing," Tonja said. But she told Karen she was going to run away.

"I wiped a tear from her eye," Karen says. "Smile, I told her. Everything will be OK. I told her to call me, but she never did."

* * *

Oxendine came home a few minutes earlier than usual. His daughter was not there. When she returned, he told her she couldn't go roller skating the next night as she had planned.

"Her eyes were always quick to tear up and she cried," Oxendine says. "But she didn't seem particularly upset. She just said, 'OK, Daddy,' and went to her room."

At 10 the next morning, Oxendine and Chris, 13, left to run some errands. Oxendine says he told Tonja to dress and clean her bedroom, that they would buy groceries after he came home. Later that day she planned to drive her aunt to Four Seasons Mall to Christmas shop. She also wanted to pick out a pair of boots her father promised to give her for Christmas.

In an hour and 10 minutes, Oxendine returned home. He tried to open the front door but it was
wedged against something. He looked down and
saw Tonja lying on the floor, her lips parted, her
head against the door. Through the opening, he
asked what was wrong.

"She shot me, Daddy," Tonja told her father.
"Help me. It hurts."

Oxendine doesn't know what his daughter
meant by these words. She died in the ambulance.

Doctors told Oxendine the bullet had entered
the right side of her abdomen, angled left, then
down, before lodging in the pelvis. But the wound
wasn't what killed Tonja Oxendine, doctors told
her father. It was loss of blood.

Later that morning, Karen called Tonja.
Either her brother or her cousin answered the
phone.

"I asked if Tonja was there and he said no,"
Karen says. "I asked when she would be home.
He said, 'Never.' "

* * *

In Tonja's bedroom, officers found two stools
positioned across from each other in a corner at
the foot of the bed. The heel of the .22 rested on
one stool, the forward portion on the other.

Police determined that Tonja sat on one stool,
steadied the rifle against the other stool and the
mattress, leaned across and pulled the trigger.
The rifle jammed between the bedpost and
mattress.

Oxendine had bought the Marlin Glenfield
.22 four years ago and kept it in a closet of the
bedroom he shares with Chris. Chris and Tonja
used the rifle for target shooting, usually at a
friend's farm in Virginia, where Chris occasionally hunted squirrels.

Besides the notebook paper in the *Encounters*
book, police found the paperback novel, *Effigies,*
on top of Tonja's dresser. It tells the story of a
rural community infiltrated by demons. In one
section, the devil overtakes the body of a 9-year-
old girl.

Crumpled in the wastebasket next to Tonja's bed were two inked letters, one to "S.N.," telling her she probably can go to her game Friday instead of the Northeast game. After a long paragraph, it ends with "I guess I'll have to break...." The words after "have to break" were erased.

The second, two pages long and rambling, was unsigned, with no name at the top. It talks of uncertain feelings and caring. "What I'm really trying to say with what I've said," it ends, "is that I love you."

A few weeks later, in the night table next to Tonja's bed, Oxendine found a birthday card that never had been sent. On the front is a wishing well surrounded by flowers. Inside, Tonja had written in cursive, "Friends always, Tonja Oxendine." Roughly printed above the signature are the words "Now I guess I hate (sic) to take you out to dinner. Anyway, happy" (the printing stops).

Inside the card was a section of a yellowed newspaper clipping Oxendine thought was still in his Bible.

"...The blast struck the woman, who was sleeping on her side on the couch, in the chest. She died almost instantly.

"Oxendine ran to a neighbor's home for help, saying, 'Help me, I shot my wife. I didn't mean to do it.'

"Lt. Lutz said he questioned the child who witnessed the shooting. The boy verified his father's story, Lutz said."

* * *

If it weren't for being told there is a large cross nearby, a stranger would likely not find Tonja's place in Lakeview Memorial Park. Until the tombstone her father ordered arrives, only a small numbered plaque marks her grave.

This cold plot of ground with no identity and the warmth of Tonja's room at home makes it seem her absence must surely be temporary. Her father, aunt and friends slowly accept that it is not, yet acceptance doesn't lessen the mystery.

"It can tear you apart," Mitchell says. "You've got this great, wonderful, marvelous person you've known all this time, and all of a sudden they're gone and you don't know why."

Oxendine continues to ask the same question each day as he visits the cemetery. Sometimes he even asks his daughter.

Observations and questions

1) Greta Tilley could have begun her story this way: "Seven weeks ago, 16-year-old Tonja Faye Oxendine killed herself in her room with a rifle. It now appears that her death was linked — at least psychologically — to the accidental shooting of her mother." That would provide a clear, conventional way of beginning a story like this. Speculate on why Tilley wrote and structured the story as she did, withholding the information about the mother until later in the story.

2) In an article entitled "Jello Journalism" (*Washington Journalism Review*, April 1982), two professors argue that reporters have gone soft in their leads, that they have forgotten the news. Read that essay and speculate on how the authors might react to Tilley's story. Are there ways that her lead could have been shortened and tightened?

3) The story begins with the phrase, "Seven weeks have passed." Does that phrase suggest that this story will be longer and more fully developed than a breaking news story on the event? What difficulties does a reporter face in writing a story seven weeks after the event?

4) Examine the story and count the number of sources that are used to shed light on the character of Tonja Oxendine.

5) What physical evidence does the reporter use to tell about the life and character of the dead girl?

6) In writing such a story, the reporter must confront serious questions about invasion of privacy.

Discuss these ethical problems: What is the purpose of telling this story? What public good does it serve? Does the reporter have the right to sit in the room of the dead girl and explore her most personal belongings, even with permission? What if family, friends and father had not agreed to tell Tonja's story? Should the reporter have proceeded?

7) An article in the *American Journal of Sociology* (December 1982) suggests that well-publicized suicides may influence others to commit suicide. A report of the Hastings Center (April 1983) asks, "Given the power of the media to evoke imitative behavior...what, if anything, ought to be done?" How would you respond to that question?

8) The writer could probably have included statistical information about the growing rate of teen-age suicides. Would such information have contributed to your understanding of the story?

9) In a way, this story has the structure of a mystery. It offers the reader an implied question: Why did this seemingly normal girl end her own life? There seems to be no clear-cut answer, although the death of her mother had a profound and mysterious effect on her. Reread this story and pay careful attention to how the writer orders the information about Tonja's life and death.

10) Examine all the elements of foreshadowing in the first section of Tilley's story. Look at the words and phrases which have connotations of death: "Seven weeks have passed"; "as Tonja left it"; "The deadline was Jan. 15"; "Signs of life"; "Each poem is about death"; "the rise in teen-age suicides"; "From now to your death." Consider how these phrases help the writer build the momentum of the story.

Greta Tilley at work

The obituary in the morning paper was brief.

She was an athlete with a list of honors after her name, including a prestigious award for character and scholarship. She died from a self-inflicted .22-caliber rifle wound. She was 16.

I read the death notice of Tonja Faye Oxendine and wanted to know more. Tonja's name signaled her Lumbee Indian heritage, so I called Ruth Revels, director of the city's Native American Association.

Coincidentally, Ruth knew Tonja. She talked about her accomplishments, her many friends, her warmth, her smile. Almost as an afterthought, she mentioned Tonja's mother had died years ago after Tonja's father shot her with a shotgun. As far as she knew, the death was accidental.

I don't believe in pushing people into stories when the choice is theirs. Either they want to talk or they don't.

Douglas Oxendine, Tonja's father, wanted to talk. I had asked Ruth to mention my interest to him and he agreed to see me.

I cautioned him that I would ask many questions, some personal, that the interviews would be painful, that he might find out some things about Tonja he didn't want to know. He said talking would be therapeutic, that he would like to uncover the reason for Tonja's death. He wanted other parents to take heed.

I didn't open my notebook that day. We talked awhile, or rather, I listened. Oxendine rambled and wasn't always coherent.

We met again a few days later and this time talked for hours. Oxendine cried, but the toughest part for me was seeing Tonja's room. It was as if she had left to run an errand and would return any minute.

Editors can be peculiar. Mine accuse me of researching ad infinitum. Don Patterson, *Record* city editor, feigned a fall from his chair when I told him I would try to have the piece ready in a week.

Bless Don, he refused the offer. If you're going to do it, he said, do it right. Something like this will be as effective six months from now as it is today.

The story took about five weeks, four for research, one for reviewing, organizing, making those "one last phone calls" and writing. By this time, editors had begun informing me they didn't expect a book. As usual, I hadn't left myself enough time in front of the terminal.

After interviewing Oxendine the second time, I decided on some personal ground rules. I wanted support for each fact or theory I heard, and decided not to use anything unless it could be verified by at least one other person. Fortunately, Tonja and her friends often corresponded through letters and notes and kept many they received. Tonja also saved letters she wrote and never sent. These stacks of letters were critical.

I wanted to know Tonja as others had known her. I don't recall how many people I interviewed, but there were dozens. Coaches, teachers, friends from school and on ball teams, relatives, neighbors, and of course, the detective who investigated the case.

Most interviews were emotional and tense. I talked to key people at least two times, usually more. I tried not to press those uneasy about opening up, but kept coming back. Some became excellent sources.

Oxendine and I spent many hours together, and though I'm sure he became weary of the tedious, often repetitive detail, he didn't complain.

I spent an afternoon in Tonja's room, perusing her belongings and thinking things through. I was a stranger with no business in this place. Why should I expose the life of a confused teen-ager who wanted peace? I almost abandoned the story.

I can't say I wrote a lead while sitting on Tonja's bed looking through her jewelry box, nor can I say I consciously structured the story in my mind. But certain things became clear.

I had become obsessed with solving the mystery of Tonja's death. I now realized months and months of research couldn't accomplish that.

I knew that for the story to be successful, the reader must know Tonja as a person. I wanted the reader to feel what I felt the first time I walked into her bedroom.

I knew the story must deal with the guilt and frustration of those left behind, and show how, even when you are looking for signals, you don't always know how to interpret them.

I knew the same thing could happen to anybody's daughter, and that if this didn't come across, the story would have failed.

I don't recall talking much with editors before writing the story. I do recall one conversation with Alfred Hamilton, then *Record* managing editor. Alfred and I have worked together enough to zero in without exchanging many words, and after I felt 75 percent certain I could begin to write (a high percentage for me), we sat in his office and chatted. No dramatic talk, just communicating to each other that appropriate bases had been touched, that information checked out, that unless I screwed up beyond all screwups, the story should be pretty good.

Two editors worked with the story before publication day, Alfred and Walter Rugaber, then *Greensboro Daily News & Record* executive editor. Alfred, as usual, walked out of his office with a printout covered with black marks and as usual, I sent him a look that only a commander in the Naval Reserve such as Alfred could take.

As usual, we sat together at the terminal, me trying to read the printout upside down and him calmly reading out words to cut. Much was tightening. He suggested we switch some paragraphs to make a time sequence less confusing and it worked. He pointed out a couple of statements that, because the evidence wasn't 100 percent sure, would be better left out.

Then we moved to the part of the story we have the most fun fooling with, the ending.

It's become a challenge. Every time I turn in a story to Alfred, I try to come up with an ending he can't touch. Many times, he brings it back with a suggestion to make it better. It's rarely a different ending and never an ending that changes the meaning. It's usually just improving what's already there. We work on the ending together until it feels right. Neither of us has ever talked about this procedure that has become habit. It would ruin the fun.

So went Tonja's ending. I had stopped the story with her father in the cemetery, but Alfred suggested some refining, and we worked on it. I still wasn't satisfied and kept returning to fiddle some more. Just before the story ran, I sneaked into the terminal one last time to change a few words, then confessed to Alfred when I figured he was too busy to care. It worked.

Walter Rugaber, as I recall, liked the beginning of the story, but wanted me to get into it more quickly. I painfully cut some things, but reading it again, I am convinced I didn't cut enough. I wanted readers to know Tonja before they saw her die but overdid the introduction.

As for other second thoughts, there are plenty. I'm still not sure about the ending. I worry about the length, though that didn't seem to concern the editors. A deadline and my delay in writing prevented me from choosing words as carefully as I would have liked. I see many sentences I could improve and needed a Rolaid after finding a "particularly interested" and a "cared deeply."

That weary cliche reminds me that I came to care deeply about a 16-year-old. Getting too close to a subject often threatens judgment. This time, it might have made judgment possible.

A conversation with
Greta Tilley

CLARK: I teach fourth and fifth graders to write. I'm interested in when and how people learn writing. Were you a writer when you were a kid?

TILLEY: I didn't think of myself as a writer, but I loved to read. I was never without a book. We never had formal family dinners where everybody had to sit together. So right through the 7th grade or so, I would take a book to the table with me and prop my knees up against the table ledge. I always had dents on my knees from the table ledge. I read while I ate. I enjoyed writing in school. I'd make good grades on my themes. Sometimes they were kind of humorous and the teachers would like that.

What did you read?

Everything. Nothing in particular. Mostly novels. We had a bookmobile that came into our neighborhood. I would get on the bookmobile every week and just pile on the books and come home and read.

Did you work on your high school newspaper?

Oh, yes. I'll tell you the honest truth. I made fairly good grades but I was kind of a slack student. I could get by without applying myself. I was sort of immature in high school, but I was very in-

Interviews were conducted and recorded over the telephone. Tapes were transcribed and edited. Some questions have been paraphrased for clarity and brevity.

terested in the high school paper. Deep down I always knew that was something I would go into. But I was not one of these students who sit down and plot out their careers.

I know a lot of good writers who were mediocre students, who got bad grades in courses they really didn't care about.

I was exactly as you describe. I went to summer school for geometry. But when it came to anything I enjoyed—especially English and literature—they would always read my themes aloud. I would write all my friends' book reports for them. I was the Teen Scene reporter for the *News and Courier* in high school and really enjoyed that.

Most people think of writing as an act of the ego. But people tell me that you are very humble and insecure about your work. Is that true?

If it is an expression of ego, it's a very unconscious one. I am such a self-doubter and a terrible judge of my own work. Editors get so frustrated with me. They'll come up to me and say, "Well, what do you have?" I always think that I don't have anything. I say to myself, "Oh, God, have I failed. This is going to be terrible." And they say to me, "Well, damn! We were going to put this at the bottom of 1B, but it belongs on the first page." I don't know, I really don't know.

Since you called and told me you were going to ask these questions, I had to sit down and say, "Well, why in the world did I win this award?" I see the writers I admire so much and I know that my style is totally different. I could never be a Saul Pett because he has such command of his stories and a command of the language. I know I don't have that and never will. Writing is not a conscious ego thing. I wish that half of my stories didn't have my name on them.

You describe yourself as a self-doubter. I'm wondering how that affects the process of writing and rewriting. How do you know your story is ready to go in the paper?

I am a procrastinator. I will over-research so that when I have a deadline, I don't leave myself enough time to write. I'm so afraid to sit down and start writing. My editor says he always knows when I'm writing because I walk past his desk every 15 minutes to go to the bathroom. And that's the truth.

So I don't give myself time to sit down and plan because they're yelling for the story. So after they edit the story, I'm always sneaking back in there (laughs). I'll read it 85 times between the time they finish editing it and the time it goes in the paper, making these little changes, worrying about did I get this right, did I get that right.

Are you planning your story while you research? Are you looking for your lead?

People say that they think about leads over and over in their heads. When I was writing on deadline for an afternoon paper, you had to write your lead on a napkin in a car because you had 45 minutes to write the story. But to tell you the truth, I am not a disciplined person or a disciplined thinker.

You live the story. You live the story from the minute you start to the minute you finish. It's always with you somewhere down there. But I'm not one of the people who say, "Now I'm going to think about a, b or c." I'm always thinking about it below the surface. When I sit down to write, I know I've thought about it, because it's kind of clear. Sometimes I'll say, "OK, here's my lead." But most of the time it turns out to be my ending, or not used at all. Or I'll say, "This is my ending," and it winds up being my lead.

Tell me about the Tonja Oxendine story. It must have been a difficult story to report and write.

Here's someone who committed suicide because she couldn't cope with something. And here you are totally invading her life. Here's some stranger getting ready to expose all these things to the world. That was my problem, plus the problem of talking to people who still hurt so much. Now for her father, it was therapeutic for him. I would not have done the story if the father had not been agreeable. I had never talked to so many people who were so emotional on a continuing basis. That was tough.

What sort of frame of mind do you have to bring as a reporter and a person to the writing of a story like this?

I've done a kind of 180-degrees on this. You think you have to be this cold person with a precise professional manner, whatever that is. And I thought that is so totally foreign to my personality. I had a conflict about it: If I go into an interview and I am myself, which is normally sympathetic, is that fair, is that ethical? At first I asked myself if it's fair to let people see how sympathetic I am, and then I said, "Well, why not?" One thing I always try to do is to tell somebody at the start why I am doing the story, what I want to do in the story. You know that I'm going to cover the good things, but I'm also going to cover the bad things, that we're going to be honest with each other. So long as you set up those terms, why not be yourself? Somebody would just burst into tears. It would be hard not to be sympathetic.

You could have written this story with a traditional lead and a conventional structure. You could have begun the story by informing the reader that a teenage girl had committed suicide with a rifle and that so

many years ago her mother had been killed accidentally with a rifle. Instead, you chose a very different structure in which the whole nature of her personality evolves in the story and where the key psychic connection—the death of her mother—is held near the end.

It never occurred to me to write it the way you read it. I wanted to give the reader the same feeling I had. I picked up the obituaries one day and there was a short obituary with a little picture about this teen-ager who had committed suicide. It listed all her activities. I thought, "Gosh, why?" So I started looking into it, and the more I started hearing about her, the more I was amazed. What has happened? What a waste.

I thought it took me too long to get into that story. It just pains me to read my stories again. I would have condensed it more if I could do it again. I would do it the same way, only shorter. I wanted my reader to get the same sense I did when I went into her room the first time. I wanted the reader to know what kind of person this was.

I think if you had used a more conventional lead, it would have reduced a very complicated and sensitive kind of story to a conventional story type. Cause and effect. When I read your story, the structure almost suggests that this 16-year-old was so complicated, and had so many emotional forces pulling in different directions, and there are no easy answers as to why this young woman, or any teen-ager, ends her life.

Bless you for saying that because that was my impression and that was what I was trying to get across.

How many people did you talk to?

Many, many, many people. Fifty at least, maybe more.

How long did that take?

Probably a month just to do the research and maybe a week to write it. I quote a lot of people. I probably quote too many people. The story is probably too long. If I could come back two weeks later, I'd probably tighten the story up. But you're so close to it. It's hard to know what to cut out.

You must have come back with a hundred pages of notes.

I have four or five legal pads at least, and then some other kinds of notes.

Out of all that material, how do you decide what you're going to use?

Some people write without looking at their notes. I try to cheat sometimes, and start writing without my notes. I'll get two or three graphs and just give up. I underline in my notes what I want to use. I always want to use too much. I'm not nearly as selective as I should be.

First I underlined key things people had to say about Tonja, a key sentence, a letter she had written, and I did it by the name of the person. Then I organized key things about Tonja herself. Then I would organize things about her father. Then I went through and took out things, because I didn't want to duplicate myself. Then I would make notes if I thought I had a hole. Then I started getting back to the typewriter or terminal. I may have also put down the different sections I wanted to have in the story. To do something like this is highly organized for me.

You use that police label. When you first saw that, did you know you would use it?

I sure did. I told the father that at some point I wanted to be in the bedroom by myself. I wanted him to let me look at everything that he felt would help. He started pouring out papers and emptying out closets and drawers. He kind of put them around me on the bed. That was when I really thought, "What am I doing here? Why am I doing this?" Then I got to this box and it had this manila envelope and it had this police tag across it. I opened it and here would be a bloody shirt. Even though you're doing it and it's real, that's when it's really real.

Where do your story ideas come from?

I very much believe in going to the library by myself—the public library. Just spending an afternoon reading, or thinking, or just sitting there daydreaming. You just need to be in a quiet place sometimes to see things. Yeah, I'll spend an afternoon just thinking, riding around, making lists.

Do you ever think about sentences? Do you say to yourself: I want this sentence to have this particular effect?

Unconsciously, yes. Consciously, no. I wish I could discipline myself to think about those things. But if I did, I might lose that tiny bit of something that I have. I may have to do a sentence 20 times before I get that one little sentence right. I'm constantly changing things. And the only way I know it's right is if it feels right.

Do you welcome editing of your copy?

Some reporters can't stand to be edited. And editors can really screw up, especially those who aren't on your wavelength and don't understand your style. But when you have an editor who respects your style, he can be so helpful. For me, some of the most fun of the whole process now is getting on the terminal with them after I've

written the story, and seeing the printout come
back with these marks on it, and seeing how
right they are, and getting together and fixing
it. I just love that.

How can an editor help you?

I'm looking for someone who can help me tighten
up without losing the sense and the feeling. If
you have an editor who has a feel for the writing,
then you feel like you can take some chances and
really try some things because they are going to
be behind you to catch you. I want them to catch
me before I make a fool of myself in the paper.
You've got to feel like you can reach for
something.

**Does anyone rap your knuckles for going in-
to the story after it's been edited?**

They tease me. They kind of know I'm gonna
sneak in there. I won't change anything unless
I talk to them about it. It's not that I doubt them.
I'm just afraid that I've gotten a name wrong,
that I could have said something a little better.
It's a joke. They say, "Greta, you have to let go
of it." But I don't want to let go of it. And it
makes me just about physically sick to read it
in the paper.

Rheta Grimsley Johnson
Commentary

RHETA GRIMSLEY JOHNSON, 30, covers Mississippi from the Jackson bureau of the *Memphis Commercial Appeal*. She writes news stories and columns. Born in rural Colquitt, Georgia, she grew up in Montgomery, Alabama, and was graduated from Auburn University in 1975 with a degree in journalism. After college she and two fellow journalism graduates started a weekly newspaper on St. Simons Island, Georgia. She later wrote for newspapers in Alabama and for UPI before joining the *Commercial Appeal* in 1980. She has never traveled north of Washington, D.C.

Bitten by his own dog

His life's patterns would make poor lyrics for a country song. For he was straight and clean-shaven, rarely drunk and less often in love.

He kept the children in shoes, his wife in Tupperware and the company car clean. He was middle class when it meant something, back when it was a state of mind and being, before it became just a vanishing socio-economic stratum.

More than three bedrooms, a bath and a half and an oil-stained carport would have been too much. His wildest fantasies were of patio awnings and an automatic charcoal starter for a portable grill. It would have been nice to get the recliner re-covered. He could survey his handkerchief-sized kingdom through sliding glass doors.

To have had any more than a 30-year mortgage and Saturdays off would have confused him. And the only confusion he allowed in his life centered on the tint knob on his color TV.

He didn't cheat on his wife or his income tax or, if he did, he didn't admit it. He only stole what was expected of him, that allowable under corporate law: an occasional day off, a pencil, a sideways look at a secretary.

For nearly 30 years he hit the road for the same company, applying a high school education, elbow grease and a frightening single-mindedness to any and all problems. He profit-shared his way to modest success, trading in his youth and then middle age for a paycheck. He sang the company song, threw the company pitch and accepted nights on the road and countless motel rooms as his life's assignment.

He was a good provider, the one thing he'd always known he must be. To stray from the straight and narrow, to stop and wonder about the grass on the other side, would have wasted time.

Sometimes late at night he'd sit alone, the glowing orange tip of his cigarette a lone spot of light in a dark suburban den. Those nights would frighten his family, would make them wonder if he had second thoughts about the irreversible course he'd charted. He quashed inner rebellion as he'd crush that cigarette, hitting the road again the next morning with shoes shined and sleeves rolled up.

He had no passions, few diversions. Music tried to lure a soul from its dark casing. He had an ear for it, but no time. Baseball brought the sparks but not the fire of emotion.

His politics were practical, timid. He wanted no blacks in school with his children, but no George Wallace sticker on his car. He worried some about going to hell but not enough to go through the hell of organized religion.

He played but one part, that of provider. His life was his job. His job was his life. Do right by the company, the company does right by you.

When he was betrayed, 25 years into his career, it was more than being passed over for a promised promotion. It was like an unfaithful spouse, an errant child, the ultimate treason. The shine was gone from his 25-year silver tray. The company had forgotten its own. He'd been bitten by his own dog.

Angry and confused, he slowed down some. He hit the road but with less force. He took off the company ring. He sold his company stock. His bitterness cost him his job.

Now, in a world where recent college graduates dare on slick printed resumes to list salary expectations, this 56-year-old man stands perplexed. Something went wrong, but he's not sure what.

As the miles wrapped themselves around his radials, he thought only of the next town, the next job. He had postponed his dreams.

It was a turn of events my father had never considered.

Observations and questions

1) By making reference to a "country song" in her lead, the writer creates an instant environment against which her father can be judged. Explore this reference. How is her father's life different from the lives described in country music?

2) This turns into an intensely personal essay. What journalistic purpose is served by telling the story of her father? Discuss the limits of this kind of writing. What topics deserve to be kept secret, even when they concern a member of the writer's family?

3) The structure of this piece turns sharply when we learn, in the final sentence, that the man is her father. If she had not revealed this, would you have the same feeling for the story? Would it have been as credible?

4) Throughout her work, Johnson uses specific, concrete objects to signify certain values: *Tupperware, company car, patio awning, charcoal starter, sliding glass door.* What do such details show us about her father?

5) This tale is told as if it were the story of Everyman, a microcosm for all people who feel betrayed by a former employer. Think of other ways in which such a story might be told. Could it have been told in an editorial or a news/feature story?

6) Read this story aloud and consider how the writer uses sounds for specific effect. Listen for the resonance of such words as *quashed, crush, shoes, shined.* Look for other interesting combinations of sound.

Roloff and his flock

NOVEMBER 10, 1982

Not all of the girls were pregnant. Some had been into drugs or shoplifting or skipping school. Some simply had parents who rued the way the world was heading and felt there must be a better way.

Most of them had an ashen look, their faces washed clean of all makeup and their budding bodies hidden under long skirts and loose blouses. They wore cheap tennis shoes with white crew socks and barrettes to keep their hair out of their eyes.

Not far away, thousands of college coeds were sunning and dreaming aloud as rock music rolled through cassettes onto the sundeck. Later, they would squeeze their trim, toasted bodies into designer jeans and greet their dates. But that was a world away from the Bethesda Home for Girls in Hattiesburg, Miss. It was at least five miles.

At Bethesda, the young girls took turns playing volleyball in the deep shade of Brother Bob Wills' neat lawn. They weren't exactly the zombie-quiet creatures described in a federal court suit the Southern Poverty Law Center filed against the home. They were farmers' daughters, happy and fat and distrustful of anything beyond the driveway.

Hard work and a disdain for the modern world were the legacies left them by Texas evangelist Lester Roloff. He had started the school and later "swapped" it with Wills for a boys' home in Tennessee.

It was still the gospel according to Roloff that was taught at Bethesda. Roloff's raspy voice on Bible study tapes was the entertainment that replaced television each night. And it was his belief that corporal punishment and hard work could save teen-age souls that Wills parroted.

Wills, an earnest, middle-aged man with a large, cowboy belt buckle holding up his jeans, had been tutored by the master.

Now Roloff is dead.

His most zealous supporters claimed the crash of a Cessna 210 over Texas flatlands last week not only killed their leader but signaled Doomsday. If so, it's a Doomsday the girls at Bethesda expected.

They had been told just how close to the fiery gates of hell they came. And most of them eventually believed.

There was a devil painted on one wall of a crowded classroom where partitions separated the 70 students. They stood on cue and sang *a cappella* anthems thanking God and Wills for their deliverance.

They took turns telling of horrible pasts, of knife fights and group sex. They cried a lot. They said they didn't ever want to leave. Yet even in daylight, the school's doors were locked.

In Texas, there is a mournful quiet where Roloff's noisy, pulpit-pounding radio broadcasts used to be. The preacher who grabbed national headlines with a nine-year legal battle to operate his homes without state licensing is dead. Accusations that some of the homes' occupants were beaten and underfed still live.

"My old daddy spanked me, and some of these girls have to be spanked, too," Roloff always said.

His battles against rock music and state regulations probably will continue. It would be bad business not to keep fighting. The homes, financed by donations, formed the basis of Roloff Enterprises, which enjoyed exemption from taxes as religious work. A few years ago, Roloff put the annual receipts at $2.5 million.

His "branch" offices in places like Bethesda are coming increasingly under fire. A preliminary injunction is still pending against Bethesda in a Montgomery, Ala., federal court. The home's population has dwindled to 20 since last April. Times are hard on the Hattiesburg ranch.

Bob Wills no longer is accommodating to strangers. But once, back when the trouble first started, he happily put the girls through their paces for visitors. He even had to curb the enthusiasm of their emotional avowals when they threatened to take up too much time.

"Oh, I beat you girls all the time, don't I?" he'd ask with a laugh. The girls laughed, too. In unison.

And then, once outside, he quit laughing. His eyes filled with tears and he told of the persecution by outsiders who didn't understand about the love that was being dispensed. He looked longingly at the groomed acreage and buses and dormitories under construction and saw heaven.

"Most of these girls had nothing when they came here. Nothing."

Then he went back inside, locking the door behind him.

Observations and questions

1) Good writers use word order to create emphasis for the reader. Read this piece to determine how Johnson uses the last words in sentences and paragraphs to deliver a final thrust at the reader:
>Not all of the girls were *pregnant*.
>...Wills *parroted*.
>...the school's doors were *locked*.
>...Roloff put the annual receipts at *$2.5 million*.
>...and saw *heaven*.

2) Johnson uses interesting and different words, but not difficult ones. Consider the word *rued* in her first paragraph. Think of some synonyms. Do they work as well as *rued?*

3) In paragraphs two and three, Johnson uses alliteration and rhyme to reinforce her commentary. Consider the repetition of the *b* sound in *budding bodies, blouses* and *barrettes.* What is the effect of the rhyming of *barrettes* with *cassettes?* Examine the use of these techniques throughout Johnson's work.

4) This story includes elements of *comparison* and *contrast.* The university, we are told, is "a world away" from the school for girls. "It was at least five miles." In what sense do those five miles equal a world? Has the writer given you enough evidence to make this point?

5) Johnson includes only two paragraphs of background on Lester Roloff. Does the information about him—his annual receipts, for example, whet your appetite for more? Would additional reporting and research make this a more important story?

A southern town with two courthouses

NOVEMBER 8, 1982

They cut down Boo Radley's oak tree in 1976 when its diseased limbs started falling faster than leaves around the heads of Monroeville, Ala., school children.

That tree was one of the last authentic props in the town where Nelle Harper Lee learned from her father it was a sin to kill a mockingbird. She won a Pulitzer Prize for trying to teach the world the same lesson.

By then, most of the houses along Alabama Avenue, including the old Lee home, already were razed and replaced by fast-food palaces, car dealerships and the mill offices of Vanity Fair. That world-famous clothier daily transformed cheap Alabama labor into a harvest of pastel undergarments with New York Fifth Avenue labels.

More Alabamians know about the Vanity Fair mill outlet store there than about the south Alabama author who gently—and with humor—poked at prejudice. The town's only physical acknowledgment of Miss Lee's literary genius is a limited, autographed supply of *To Kill A Mockingbird* in the downtown religious book store. There the books are stacked alongside Anita Bryant's life story and Debby Boone sheet music.

There are no libraries or roads named in her honor. No one wonders aloud any longer about what she'll write next. It even took a stubborn stand by history buffs to keep the old courthouse intact when county business outgrew it.

It persists in the square, though, with a new courthouse now right beside it. Old men, just as persistent as the structure shadowing them, play a continuing game of dominoes in a white outbuilding. The old and the new form a narrow alley across the grounds where Harper Lee once romped with her growing imagination.

For years, Mary Ida Carter was caretaker at the Old Courthouse Museum. She was one of those people who make fictional characters seem dull. A Yankee writer from Harper's ran into Miss Carter one day, discounting her in print as "a languid old woman who claimed to be Truman Capote's aunt." She was Capote's aunt, one of several who kept him on a seasonal basis during most of his childhood.

It was during those hot, south Alabama summers together that Capote and Miss Lee became friends bound by a love of words and a recognition, yet forgiveness, of Southern faults. The character Dill in Miss Lee's semi-autobiographical book was based on Capote. Several of his short stories, including "A Christmas Memory," have Monroeville backdrops.

There are literary experts everywhere in Monroeville. Just ask them. Some say Nelle—the town calls her Nelle—exhausted her childhood memories in *To Kill A Mockingbird* and that's why she's never finished anything else. Others say Capote wrote—or heavily edited—her one, lauded novel. Others say she had a heavy hand in his stories. A few say they've never read the nonsense.

Harper Lee comes home now periodically to visit her sister, lawyer Alice Lee, who is as civic-minded and outgoing as Harper is reclusive. One doesn't hear that Nelle's in town; only that she just left.

The town's still a little miffed at her portrayal. The Lady's Society and missionary tea mentality that marked Maycomb, her fictionalized Monroeville, still is alive and well and pouring watered-down punch. Polite society is quick to claim Harper Lee, but they stress the vanishing landmarks and ignore the poignant attacks on hypocrisy that made the book a classic.

Worldwide attention helped the town get over its first anger. The Hollywood set-makers came to town to copy the courtroom, adding a rail or two to the outside of the edifice but making an exact interior reproduction. They studied angles and arches; Gregory Peck studied ambience.

Peck spent a few days there to prepare for his Atticus Finch role, and that visit's something the town considers real scrapbook material.

A local bank teller looked up from counting bills one day to stare into Peck's celebrated face. He presented a check for several hundred dollars and asked to cash it. "I don't think I'll cash it, Mr. Peck." the star-struck teller said, "I think I'll just keep it."

"That," Peck's supposed to have said, "will be just dandy."

Then the movie was released, its courageous Atticus Finch defending a black man accused of raping a white woman right there on the giant screen, and the quiet resentment came again.

It's a town that still has more stop lights than Catholics and where newcomers are held at arm's length until they prove themselves. An all-black section several miles from town always is referred to as Clausell Quarters. The Atticus Finches still are grossly outnumbered. They still are objects of curiosity, if no longer hate.

But to deny a celebrity—even one like Harper Lee, whose spotlight faded years ago—is not easy in a town the size of Monroeville. There is a grudging respect for the woman who is one of them, yet apart. They have forgiven her for making good and for telling the truth in a prize-winning way.

Observations and questions

1) Read the paragraph beginning "The town's still a little miffed at her portrayal." Notice the extensive alliteration throughout that paragraph, the repetition of *m*s and *p*s. Does this add to the pleasure of reading, or do you find it excessive and self-indulgent?

2) The writer claims her own work was influenced by the work of Harper Lee. Read *To Kill a Mockingbird*. What lines of influence can you detect?

3) Every writer eventually faces the challenge of how to describe the general characteristics of a community without descent into stereotype. How does Johnson meet that challenge? Is she fair to the residents of Monroeville?

4) Johnson derives commentary from description and observation. What level of commentary is present in the sentence: "There the books are stacked alongside Anita Bryant's life story and Debby Boone sheet music"?

Past tenses, future spouses

DECEMBER 24, 1982

The imprint of a chenille bedspread marks her face. She has been napping.

It is dusk now, and the cold, fogged window panes rattle as she walks toward her rocking chair. The free-swinging yellow light bulb makes strange shadows across a bowl of wax fruit that has faded from age and the south Georgia sunshine. It's a few days before Christmas, but it won't be the same without him.

His name was Clifford Houston, and she has been alone since the hot day when somber men in dark suits brought him up steps he had built to this room. It was here they held the emotional, open-casket vigil that's obligatory in the Deep South. It was then that she began living her life in the past tense.

He was a farmer and she was his wife. That was their story.

God knows he wasn't perfect. But he brought her the food she cooked and was kind to her when she was sick. With advanced age came a tenderness that would prompt him to help with the cooking or dishes. She was his helpmate and that was enough.

Their union had been complete, forged by the years and hard times and four children. She had never learned to drive or plow, but then he had never learned to make a bed or sew.

She wasn't pampered. Far from it. The same small hands that crocheted intricate patterns wrung the necks of the chickens she fried. She routinely dispatched snakes with her small garden hoe.

A meal too elaborate ever to be called lunch was on the table every noon, and it appeased the appetites of a family of field hands. He was out before dawn, farming or building windmills or paving roads for $1 a day. There was a simple division of duties that neither of them challenged. They were partners in survival.

At night they snored in unison.

Now she is simply marking time in a room where it's always late afternoon.

* * *

In a small town outside of Denver, a man takes a wife. She is his third.

The chapel has a rustic exterior and plush interior and a picture window to look out at the mountains. JoAnne is dressed in a formal white gown and John wears a dress suit and cowboy boots. Her long hair has been French braided by a hairdresser, framing smooth skin and prominent cheek bones.

A Christmas tree decorates the church, and carols and fine wine lift the spirits of the guests.

They are a handsome couple. Between them, they have several degrees and three former spouses. They have a nice home and the chance for a beautiful life in a land populated by mostly beautiful people who take ski lessons and buy season symphony tickets.

The bride, today, has the hopeful look of a teen-ager selecting a used car from a crowded lot. She sees only the shiny new paint jobs and no rusted engines. She wants to believe this is it.

Her medical career won't suffer from this new marriage. The bridegroom has promised to be accommodating. They will share household duties and measure their happiness by the inches of snow on the slopes. They will have a modern marriage.

We have come so far, we women who wanted more than marriage and mate. Those of us who do marry, do so almost incidentally. Like sexual power brokers, we wrestle all sorts of marital concessions from our spouses before walking the aisle. We say "You will" and not "I do."

The exchange women made has been a good one, in most respects. The inevitability of recognizing women as full-fledged people really leaves us little room to mourn the passing of a completely submissive love, no matter how appealing it looks in its simplicity.

Yet the beautiful Denver bride who also is a smart young doctor basically wants from life what her grandmother had. Happiness. She hasn't found it in a promising career or with trips to warm exotic beaches. She is a feminist who still wants to love and be loved.

Perhaps now she marries the man she will mourn.

For like her grandmother before her, she doesn't want to be alone at Christmas.

Observations and questions

1)   The first two paragraphs are written in the present tense. Johnson suddenly shifts into the past: "His name was Clifford Houston." The same paragraph says "It was then that she began living her life in the past tense." What is the effect of such a technique on the reader? Is it too blatantly rhetorical? Is it a flourish without a purpose?

2)   This column veers when the author says, "We have come so far, we women who wanted more than marriage and mate." Is the injection of the first person an intrusion here? Discuss the shift at that point from description to exposition.

3)   The two women in this column are related to the writer, grandmother and sister. Does knowing this change your feelings about the story?

4)   Johnson uses no quotations in this story and uses them sparingly throughout her commentary. Most journalists look for opportunities to get other human voices into their stories. Does the absence of such voices detract from these columns?

5)   How much credibility does a name lend to a story? Are there some stories that must be told even though names cannot be used? Are you distrustful of stories that derive from anonymous sources or use fictitious names?

A good and peaceful reputation

NOVEMBER 1, 1982

It seemed like a family reunion. Like a ritual gathering deep in the country where there are no secrets or pretenses and the black sheep break bread and belch loudly with the rest of the clan. The children run barefoot and unchecked and old men spit wherever they please as acceptance prevails.

That's sort of the way it was. Relatives huddled around a prodigal son who grudgingly put in an appearance.

The women wore tentative smiles with their Dacron summer finery and carried patent leather bags on arms the Mississippi sun had mottled.

The men held back to avoid the endless hugging and to clear their throats. Then, those not desperate for a smoke moved in with handshakes and conspiratorial winks and whispered reassurances for their white friend and neighbor who had shot and killed a black deputy sheriff.

It was a somber, special occasion. A funeral where everyone got to speak to the corpse.

At each brief recess, the crowded courtroom seemed to shift forward as a high tide of women lapped around defendant Jimmy Lancaster of Van Vleet. He smiled a weak smile summoned from somewhere in his uncomplicated past and allowed himself to be pressed and pitied. He knew his role.

Lancaster periodically fingered his wide, polyester lapels to find and fasten the missing galluses. The suit was a strange new uniform for the jail-paled, lanky welder who liked to hunt and keep to himself. He held his head stiffly erect, as if his shirt collar pinched and there was no polite way to loosen it. He had the self-conscious look of someone posing for a Polaroid.

His supporters might not comprehend the seriousness of the offense; months in jail had almost convinced Lancaster. Still, here with a forgiving family and well-wishers cooing over him, even Lancaster must have found new hope.

If the district attorney wanted to avoid the case and the considerable controversy it generated, he didn't let on, leading the prosecution with the barely-bridled ferocity of a Baptist preacher. He made the most of bloody clothing and color photographs of the victim; there was nothing half-hearted or cavalier in his manner.

The black man's law enforcement ties made it more respectable to aggressively prosecute a white man for the murder, but it still wasn't politic.

And the state's confidence was mostly superficial. They had a dead deputy and the man who said he shot him eight times in self-defense. But they had only one black on a Chickasaw County jury that came from and would return to a largely segregated society.

Lancaster told his story. Robert Kirby had come to the front door of his home early one morning, ringing the doorbell and then waiting. When he answered the door and asked what the deputy wanted, Kirby for no apparent reason shot up from his hip, through the bottom of his holster and the glass storm door.

Only grazed, Lancaster told how he grabbed a rifle and started firing at the fleeing deputy. For a better aim, he dropped one gun and went for his powerful 7mm hunting rifle that had a scope.

At least eight rounds later—after he saw Kirby's body bounce from the impact of bullets— Lancaster said he felt a little sick and went back inside.

The district attorney pulled an undamaged holster from Kirby's stained clothing to refute the Lancaster story. The defendant was slightly injured by flying glass from his own shots through the storm door, not one of Kirby's bullets, he said.

Kirby was trying to do his job.

He was trying to deliver an assault warrant filed against Lancaster by his wife who had the day before provoked a beating.

A parade of character witnesses attested to Lancaster's good and peaceful reputation. A Methodist minister, a farmer, a shop foreman and an elderly, former justice court judge all took Lancaster's part. One such witness was the employer of a white juror. In the audience, reporters could hear other testaments to Lancaster's worth. "He deserves a medal," one man said, sniffing at no one in particular.

Robert Kirby couldn't demand justice. That was in the hands of a white district attorney who must worry about re-election. It was in the purview of a white judge. It was up to a mostly white jury whose friends sat on the white side of a distinctly black and white courtroom.

Dick Gregory wasn't there. There were no banners or rallies or network television cameras. There was a crowd, but it was composed of local folks who waited for a verdict.

The widow of the slain deputy waited, too, across a narrow aisle from Lancaster's supporters. Her husband had been brash enough to interrupt a white family's feuding. And he'd gotten himself shot.

After the trial, Robert Kirby's widow went home alone. The friends of Jimmy Lancaster disbanded.

The jurors went back to their homes in towns where not much changes, and progress must be diluted and served up in small doses. They had been drafted to serve justice and now were coming home from a war with their own consciences.

They had looked down the barrel of Lancaster's rifle and seen the moment of one man's death and another man's madness. The oath they'd taken to uphold that truth mattered more than peer pressure or the politics of race. It mattered more than some unspoken allegiance to a past pockmarked by prejudice. They had been color-blinded by the truth.

In Mississippi, there are two men serving life sentences for killing blacks. One of them is Jimmy Lancaster.

Observations and questions

1) Examine Johnson's metaphoric language in the lead. Before we even learn that a trial is going on, we have the words *family reunion, ritual gathering, deep in the country, black sheep break bread and belch, the clan, barefoot,* and *spit.* What kind of mood is set by such language?

2) We are told at the end of the first paragraph that "old men spit wherever they please as acceptance prevails." That is a peculiar turn of phrase, a contradiction that embodies a social truth. Does that phrase have any thematic application to the rest of the story?

3) Johnson believes in showing, not telling. Most of her commentary is embedded in narration or observation, in sentences like "He knew his role." Where else in this story does the writer comment through description and narration?

4) The news hook comes at the end of the fourth paragraph: "...for their white friend and neighbor who had shot and killed a black deputy sheriff." Is that high enough in the story? As you discuss this, remember that this commentary was written after the news stories of the event.

5) This writer recognizes the effectiveness of active verbs. The children *run,* old men *spit,* the women *wore,* a high tide of women *lapped,* Lancaster *fingered.* Examine your own writing. Do you use active verbs? Or do you rely too heavily on the passive voice and the verb "to be"?

6) A courtroom is a good place for a reporter to be sensitive to body language. The reporter can observe people during a trial and record their

reactions to other people and events. We are told, for example, that the defendant has "the self-conscious look of someone posing for a Polaroid." Examine other instances in which the writer describes body language effectively. Are there any dangers inherent in this type of description?

7)   The writer says she likes to reward the reader with "a kicker," an off-beat or surprising ending. Reread all of Johnson's endings. Do you feel rewarded by them? In what sense?

Rheta Grimsley Johnson at work

Something about the Jimmy Lancaster trial had been bothering me for months when I finally sat down and wrote "A Good and Peaceful Reputation."

My notes from the trial already had been relegated to the cardboard box that always makes the move but never gets unpacked. My office, my assignment, my daily duties with *The Commercial Appeal* all had been changed since I reported Lancaster's conviction. Yet the week's stay in a North Mississippi courtroom remained vividly with me, its surrealistic qualities stamped permanently in that portion of the brain reserved for nagging thoughts.

It had been, from the beginning, a story that eluded print. Oh, I had reported dutifully the strategies of the prosecution and defense and described in some detail the crowded, racially-divided courtroom. With every day's story, though, there came the feeling I'd managed to ignore as much truth as I imparted. I had covered the seventh game of the World Series and omitted the score.

For there had been a crowd of people there who simply did not believe killing a black man was enough to blot a solid citizen's reputation. A preacher, a former judge and Lancaster's boss all had taken the stand to say as much.

The South is full of people who are wise and good and kind in most respects but wear bigotry like a scar on their humanity. That fact wasn't news.

"I killed, but I'm not a killer," Lancaster told that jury. That was good, Chickasaw County, Mississippi, logic. It wasn't news.

The jury didn't buy it. Intimidated as the jurors were by their white friends and neighbors and bosses seated in that courtroom, they remembered their oath. That was news, and news that begged for commentary.

The way my straight news stories read, it didn't seem remarkable that a present-day jury, even in rural Mississippi, would convict a man who admitted killing any officer of the law. That's why those news stories didn't read true.

On a good day, even in isolated, backward pockets of the South, there can be justice. And progress plows under the heavy underbrush of prejudice at a slow but steady pace.

As a native and life-time resident of the Deep South who chose reporting as a career, I have made more disillusioning treks across the region's blind spots than I'd ever counted on making. I had longed to write things are changing, things are better, but so often I couldn't convince even myself. The Jimmy Lancaster trial gave me the chance.

At the time I actually wrote the column, another trial was under way in Mississippi and getting the nationwide attention the Lancaster case had not attracted. The former black mayor of Tchula, Mississippi, Eddie Carthan, was accused of hiring outsiders to kill a black political rival. He already had been convicted of making false statements to obtain a bank loan and assaulting a policeman. Pending against him were unrelated federal charges that accused him of stealing from a federally funded poverty meals program.

Because he was black and being tried in Mississippi, many assumed he could not get a fair trial. Dick Gregory led marches. National church organizations raised funds. Local folks, both black and white, fumed. It seemed important to offer a specific, optimistic example of Southern justice.

The piece was easy to write. I sat down at the VDT late one afternoon and put down several months' worth of thoughts. Editor Michael Grehl warned me about assuming the reader understood my point without stating, in so many words, the story's moral. At his suggestion, I added the "color-blinded by the truth" phrase. It helped.

Calling the state attorney general's office to find out exactly how many convictions there had been in the state for the murder of blacks was an afterthought. The statistic summed up the case's importance in one, understated breath. It also provided a dramatic kicker and a way to let the reader hear the same surprise verdict I'd heard that summer's day in the courtroom.

I wanted the readers, even those who had read the news accounts, to be surprised again, to be sufficiently impressed with the moment's significance and, frankly, to feel encouraged.

A conversation with
Rheta Grimsley Johnson

CLARK: What is it about the South that has created both interesting literature and provocative journalism?

JOHNSON: I'm afraid my response wouldn't be very balanced. I was born in the South, grew up in the South and work in the South. I've never even visited north of Washington, D.C. People are always asking why the South, especially Mississippi, has produced so many writers.

I thought "A Good and Peaceful Reputation" had the feel of Southern literature.

I enjoyed writing that piece. For the last eight years, I have been primarily a reporter, not a columnist. I covered the straight news accounts of that story and wrote the column later. There have been so many times that I have been disillusioned about the South. I love the South. It's all I've ever known.

It would always worry me that people that I respected and that I knew to be wise and good would have these blind spots of prejudice. That's worried me all my adult life. That's why, when I see something like I saw in Chickasaw County, a rural isolated pocket in north Mississippi, where justice prevailed, it was like an awakening. These people couldn't deny the truth. It made me feel good that change eventually seeps in.

The contrasts are so vivid in the South. You have the very rich and the very poor. Whenever things are vivid, it inspires writers.

I lived in Montgomery, Alabama, for three years. I sensed there that change was not only possible in the South, but that it had been accomplished in important ways.

The South has always been the battleground for social change. It carried the primary responsibility of accomplishing this change while all the world watched. It fell on its face, no doubt, with the dogs and the fire hoses. But it has made slow progress.

I understand that you have been influenced by Southern writers like Carson McCullers, Flannery O'Connor and Harper Lee. Are those the people you grew up reading? Have they shaped your writing?

I think they influenced my philosophy more than my writing. I think it would be presumptuous to compare my style to theirs. *To Kill a Mockingbird* pointed out all the things we've been talking about: the prejudice and the hypocrisy in the South, but it did it in such a gentle way, in a loving way really. Southerners are married to their environment for better or worse.

I'm interested in the way literature influences the work of writers and the style of writers. Did you ever find yourself sitting down and trying to copy the style of a writer you admired?

Only one. This is kind of strange, but it was Raymond Chandler. He's one of my favorites and I didn't discover him until I was a senior in college. I had never read any detective stories. But the way he could turn a phrase, and his description and images were so good. If I have ever wished I could write like somebody, it would be Raymond Chandler. He got it down where people could understand it. He used everyday images, not highfalutin allusions. I found myself writing shorter sentences after I started reading a lot of Chandler. He is so short and clear. I think it helped my style. The rhythm of his work more than anything else.

Do you think consciously about the length and rhythms of your sentences?

I have two work modes. If things are going well for me, if it's coming smoothly, I don't have to think about it. It's like I'm writing with my fingers instead of my head. It just comes. If I have to struggle, which happens about 50 percent of the time, I do think about it. And I work at it. It's torturous. Usually those things are not nearly as well written. They are not the ones that win a prize (laughs). But the things I do that are good are usually the ones that come easily. It's like singing or something. It sounds right. It's so easy that it's almost scary. But it doesn't happen all the time. I'm in a terrible rut right now.

Do you know when you're working on a story which mode you're working in?

Yes, I know. I know people talk about spending a great deal of time on their leads. But unless I have my first phrase, or first sentence, the rest doesn't come.

Do you actually not write the rest of the piece until you have the first sentence? When some writers get into that predicament, they lower their standards, write a draft and go back and work on the lead.

I do that on deadline when I have to get a piece in. But I prefer not to. I prefer to have the first thought complete and sounding good, and know it's what I want to say, and the rest of the piece just comes.

How do you get that first thought? Are you always looking for it from the time you get the assignment?

I'm basically a reporter. I'll go out and cover a story and sometimes in the course of the inter-

view, driving back, or after I've already filed a
news account, if the story has made an impression on me, there will be one thing that sticks
with me.

**A friend of mine calls this process
"rehearsal." If you're driving back to the
office on deadline, you click off the radio and
see what's happening in your head. If I
rehearse well enough, when I sit down, I
make much better use of time.**

That's exactly it. The piece I wrote about my
father and unemployment: I had been on some
story assignment, totally unrelated, and was
driving back. I had promised to turn in a column.
I wrote that piece in my head driving back, about
an hour's drive. I wrote it in my head and was
probably speeding back to the office to put it
down on paper. I probably write the first part of
a story in my head as much as on paper.

**I was very taken by the effective way you
use sounds in your writing. I think Spiro
Agnew probably spoiled alliteration for
Americans for years to come. You use it sub-
tly. I didn't realize you were using it until I
started reading your prose word for word
with a pencil.**

I've always liked alliterative sounds, even in
names. I've always felt that girls in school who
had names like Cathy Cadell and Mary Maples
would be charming and popular (laughs). So I just
loved alliteration. I probably overuse it. I love
the sounds of words. There's one exact word that
you need to use and want to use, and you search
till you find it.

**How does that search come about?
Remember, you talk about well-wishers
"cooing" over Jimmy Lancaster. It seems
like the perfect word. You say a high tide of**

women "lapped" around the defendant.
Those words are startling and effective.
Where do they come from?

The verb *lapped*. I remember sitting there in
court. For some reason they had three recesses in
about two hours. The crowd would go forward and
back, almost like the tide.

So it came from observation?

That one did. Verbs are so important. I probably
did work to get *cooing*. I do go back and do a good
bit of rewriting, and that is the sort of thing I do.
I'll look for a better verb or a better descriptive
phrase.
  I don't have very much confidence in myself
as a writer, and for many reasons I don't like to
read the stuff once it's in print. I second guess
everything I do. My lack of confidence even affects
my style. I'll try to use a kicker at the end. I think
I do that to reward the reader who made it all the
way through my piece (laughs).

What sort of things do you look for during the
rewriting process?

I make sure I didn't run the reader out of breath
with long sentences.

Because of Raymond Chandler?

Right. (Laughs). In the Chickasaw County piece,
I had a good strong beginning. And the end I liked. In the middle, when I was giving an account
of what happened, I should have worked harder
on making that interesting. I was just trying to
get that over with. Sometimes I'll do that. I'll need
to throw some facts in there.

The boring but important stuff.

I'll literally throw them in to get it over with. And
then I get back to the fun part, the descrip-

tive part. So I have to watch myself there. I get carried away with the meaning and the description, and I don't work hard enough at making the meat of the matter just as fine in my writing.

Do you have your endings in mind when you begin writing the piece?

The piece on my father, for instance, I wrote the first version without saying he was my father. Then I decided it would be a stronger ending if I did, if I said here is the story of Everyman, but at the end say it was my father.

I usually don't have a conclusion in mind. I usually write myself to a conclusion more than anything else. When I start out I have to have the first sentence, that first thought, but I usually don't know how in the world I'm going to end it.

Even in the trial piece, after I had finished it, I called the attorney general's office to see if this was the first time a white man had been convicted for shooting a black man. It gave me a better ending than what I had.

I've read that you write stories about people who are not regularly interviewed, who have never been in the news before. That you tend to prefer farmers in the fields and drivers at truck stops to usual news sources. Is that true?

It seems I have never gotten a good story from an official source. It has been a detriment to my reporting that I was not able to draw out of people in high places very good quotes. I could turn around and get more information from a secretary.

There's also something perverse in me, that if everybody is writing about the unemployed, homeless bum on the street who lives in his car, I want to take a different approach. When everybody else stops writing about civil rights, I'll want to jump right in and do it.

I covered Bear Bryant's funeral. Everybody was interviewing the athletic director, the sports heroes, the coaches. I went to truck stops around Tuscaloosa. I tried to talk to people who had never seen him, but told me all they knew and then some. There is a whole portion of people who are never written about. They are not rich or in high places.

I worry sometimes about writing about people who don't understand what it means to be in a newspaper. I feel protective of these people. I want to get their words and feelings in print, but at the same time I'm worried about how they are going to react. I'm worried about what their neighbors are going to say.

I'm worried about exploiting them. I'm sure I have embarrassed some people in print. And I think your obligation goes beyond identifying yourself. I think you have to look back at what you've written. Compassion is involved. It's hard to decide where good reporting and compassion can meet. I don't approach it in a condescending way. I think that they have on any given subject the best, truest sense of what's happening. They are ignored the most. They probably make the most sense in what they say.

Where did you find the granddaughter and grandmother in your story on marriage?

The people are my sister and my grandmother. They were easy to find.

You didn't say that in the piece.

No, and it's why I didn't say my father was my father in the first version. I don't like columns that say, "I, I, me, my family." These are the only family members I have ever written about.

I felt their story was universal enough that it merited telling. It didn't matter that they were related to me.

Perhaps because of the Janet Cooke affair, some people look at literary journalism with a suspicious eye. They are suspicious of stories about unnamed people. If you had just talked about this man, and you had not said it was your father, then your story may have had less credibility with the reader.

I agree. I think it always weakens the piece when you don't use a full name when its possible. I used first names in that grandmother/granddaughter piece to begin with. Then my editor asked me to go back and use the full name of the dead man. I think he was right. The more full names you can get in a piece, the more specific you can be, the stronger the story.

I guess I'm just tired of stories that begin "Denise (not her real name)."

You just wonder, "Well, is this her real story?" I did a column on divorce that got a lot of comment from readers. I did not use names. It was "he" and "she" all the way. I couldn't see any way around that to tell a tale as personal as I told. You can't always use names and have effective pieces on some subjects.

How did your dad respond to the unemployment piece?

As far as I know, he hasn't seen it. I haven't hidden it from him. I don't think he'd like it much, actually. It's probably the hardest thing I've ever written. It's also gotten more response than anything I've ever written. I knew the tale was universal, but I got five or six letters from people with similar tales. I got dozens of letters about the column. I thought it was important to write, so I wrote it.

What I admire in your columns is that you do a lot of showing rather than telling. Your commentary is a function of your descriptive reporting. Do you think that is a valid observation?

It stems from my confidence problem. I feel rather pompous telling people what to think. I usually have a good idea what I think. But I'd rather let them figure it out. I'd rather say: this is how the scene was and this is what happened, and draw your own conclusions.

I'm intrigued by your candid expressions of insecurity, your lack of confidence. In a way it violates the stereotype that people have of talented writers, that it's all ego, that they are all prima donnas. Do you feel any better about your own work having received this award?

They called me the other day about participating in a panel discussion out in Denver (at the ASNE convention). I told the secretary, half kiddingly, that I thought she was calling to take the award back.

I know that what I write is good to the extent that readers like it. I get a lot of response from people who read the newspaper and that's really the main point anyway. And I think I know what people like to read about. But the award, if anything, has put me in a dry spell. It's made me worry that now I'll really have to be good.

Orland Dodson
Business Writing

ORLAND DODSON, 57, is business editor of the *Shreveport Times*. He joined the staff in 1975 as an investigative reporter after long experience in radio, television and newspapers. He began his career in 1943, working on a number of newspapers in Texas. He was appointed news editor of KGBC, a radio station in Galveston, in 1947. That year, he did extensive coverage of the Texas City disaster, in which more than 600 lives were lost in the harbor explosion of a ship carrying ammonium nitrate. From 1950 to 1975 he moved from newspapers to television news in Texas and Louisiana. He is a native of Plain Dealing, Louisiana.

'They' hold up interest rates

JUNE 20, 1982

Talk to a typical businessman about the economic outlook and he'll tell you that he's expecting things to begin to take on a rosier glow as soon as "they" get the interest rates down.

Bankers and savings and loan executives will tell you the same thing, and their tears are not crocodile tears. The two have to pay interest as well as collect it.

"They" to many bankers would include the brokers who are pushing money market funds. But brokers, who also deal in stocks and bonds, claim to be unhappy about interest rates, too.

High interest rates are blamed for automobiles not selling, the doldrums into which housing has fallen and the lethargy in the stock market.

And everybody blames "the Fed," the nickname of the Federal Reserve System, for a policy which is, at least by comparison with the go-go days of years gone by, tight-fisted.

Even the government blames the Fed. The secretary of the treasury and numerous congressional committees are among its frequent critics.

There's a question about the Fed, which sits at the top of the heap of the private banking system, but which bankers consider to be an arm of the government.

The chairman of the Fed, Paul Volcker, has more or less admitted that interest levels are too high for there to be a robust economic recovery of the kind most everybody seems to want.

But the Fed has no magic wand to set things right, he said, because if it relaxed its tight money policy, interest rates might edge down a bit, but they would be carried up to even higher levels on the waves of inflation, which he said would come from that relaxation.

If the bankers are not "they," and the Fed is not "they," and the government is not "they," who are "they"?

Say you have a new Individual Retirement Account, or a certificate of deposit at your bank or your savings and loan, or shares in a credit union, or a money market certificate.

Then, you are "they."

Try this exercise: Call up your banker or your broker and tell him you believe interest rates are too high and you'd like him to stop paying you 14 percent, or the current rate on T-bills, and send you 8 percent instead.

Go ahead.

All you have to do is pick up the telephone and call.

Why aren't your fingers walking to the phone?

You know, don't you?

You couldn't bring yourself to do that unless somebody was holding a gun to your head or threatening to break both your legs.

And neither could anybody else.

You might convince yourself, of course, that the stock market is sold far below value and that it might be a good time to buy in for the long bull market that's sure to come, or at least almost sure.

But probably not today.

Whoever "they" are, they've been socking money away. Money market funds, which nobody had heard about a few years ago, now have some $200 billion in deposits.

"Where would that have come from," asked a Shreveport banker, "except from the banks and the savings and loans?"

Not everybody agrees with that. Many investors would be in the stock market instead of the money markets, brokers say, except that stock hasn't been paying nearly so well.

Despite remarkable growth, the money market funds don't have it all. Banks and savings and loans are piling up new time deposits as well.

The Federal Land Bank of Atlanta recently published comparisons, May to May, on the total deposits of commercial banks and savings and loans, which showed time deposits are up significantly over last year.

The commercial banks had an increase of $27 billion in time deposits and the savings and loans gained $22 billion during the same time.

By last month, the figures showed, "they" had a total of $659 billion in time deposits at commercial banks and $426 billion at the S&Ls.

Add in the $200 billion estimated to be in the money markets, and it all amounts to $1.285 trillion, a figure as imposing as the federal debt.

The "theys" collecting on that mountain of savings really can't be expected to give up high interest rates voluntarily. But, of course, there is another side to the equation. There is another set of "theys," the ones who are paying the interest.

But they can't change things by a telephone call. These "theys" can get out of the interest rates only by paying off their debts or taking bankruptcy. Few could do the former and most hope to avoid the latter.

Classical economic theory holds that the cost of borrowing money, like the cost of potatoes, eventually is determined by the law of supply and demand.

The supply is growing, and the more rapidly because the rates are far above the rate of inflation and the compound interest rolls into the principal.

On the day when there is more money looking for borrowers than there are borrowers looking for loans, the "theys" who borrow will begin to enforce their idea of a proper interest rate on the "theys" who hold the cash.

Observations and questions

1) Dodson builds each of his columns around a strong organizing principle, a focus, a center of gravity. The heart of this column is the word "they." Who are "they"? The word appears in the title and is repeated throughout. Reread the column and examine how the writer links all elements to this single word.

2) These columns are examples of what Gene Patterson, editor of the *St. Petersburg Times*, calls "explanatory journalism." Complicated issues are explained for a general audience without resorting to jargon. The question of what keeps interest rates up is of importance to any American, especially if he or she is trying to buy a house or a car. Do you have a better sense of how various economic forces work having read this column? Can you make a list of things you still don't understand?

3) It has been said that the word "you" turns a newspaper story into a sermon. Dodson uses the word throughout this column, addressing the reader directly, even encouraging the reader to "Try this exercise." How do you respond to this as a reader?

4) Dodson avoids numbers in this story, except for three paragraphs near the end. Does he provide the reader with enough hard information to support his point?

An economic mystery: Who did Uncle Sam in?

OCTOBER 17, 1982

Who drove the richest nation on earth deep into debt, saddling it with inflation and forcing it out of the front rank of competition for excellence and productivity in the marketplace?

A succession of blundering governments? One or more unwise presidents? Congress, the bureaucrats, special interest groups lobbying for subsidies, tax shelters and special advantages?

Who destroyed the buying power of the dollar? Brought on high interest rates? Set the stage for a scary recession that has conjured up memories of the Great Depression of a half century ago and sent the splendid old industries reeling into a morass of layoffs, shutdowns and bankruptcy?

What happened to the American dream that seemed so visible and achievable in the 1950s, when the United States stood at the pinnacle of power, prestige and prosperity?

There would be a split-level house for every family, two cars for every garage, private planes for all brave enough to fly them, TVs and washing machines, carpets on the floor, pictures on the wall and plenty of leisure to enjoy these and other amenities.

Nobody snickered when there was talk of making the world over in the American image. Most every nation that counted, or hoped someday to do so, sent its leaders to Washington for advice and economic assistance to make it happen.

There was a recession in the late '50s, in the second term of President Dwight Eisenhower. The president went on the air with a one-word message to his fellow Americans.

"Buy," said Ike. Consumers, confident the president would not mislead them, went out and bought. And the recession withered away.

It hasn't been so easy lately. And the nature of the malady is harder to define. Uncle Sam is deep in debt, the U.S. industrial plant has difficulty competing with upstarts from overseas, and a ruinous inflation rate that ate away at his vitals during the '70s is coming reluctantly into check only at the cost of high interest and an unsettling rate of unemployment.

Who did Uncle Sam in? The question intrigued Dr. James Robert Michael, research director of the College of Administration and Business at Louisiana Tech University, who wondered if the answer might be tucked away unnoticed in the great mass of figures and computer data from the U.S. Bureau of Economic Analysis, for which Tech is a regional depository.

There was no shortage of suspects. Some of the most frequently accused are these:

• A huge, growing and unmanageable national debt, made worse each year by huge deficits in the government's accounts.

• High costs of American labor, fueled by unrealistic expectations that anyone who held a job owned a ticket to a ride in the middle class.

• Greedy corporations, piling up atrocious profits regardless of performance.

Michael went for the hard figures to determine what happened to these components of the economy from 1960, when the consensus was that all was well with the American economy, and 1980, by which time most everyone would agree it was in serious trouble.

Some of his findings were surprising.

For example, the level of the national debt did grow spectacularly during those two decades, by 214 percent.

But this paled by comparison with the rate at which private citizens plunged themselves into debt, by 700 percent on mortgages and by 494 percent on credit cards and other consumer debt.

Debt is doubtless a problem, especially at the kind of interest rates now commonplace. But if the federal government was plunging recklessly into debt, it was being clearly outstripped by the American people in their own private lives.

The rate of spending, of money earned or money borrowed, was also growing less swiftly at the federal level than at the state or local level. As federal spending rose by 484 percent, that of the lower levels of government went up by 618 percent.

Indeed, a significant part of the increased federal spending was revenue sharing—taxes collected by the federal government and parceled out to states and localities.

What, then, of the insatiable demands of labor, often blamed for the inflated prices and for loss of the once formidable edge U.S. products had in the world marketplace?

Wages and salaries grew very handsomely, by 484 percent, during the 20 years Michael chose to study. But the share of the pie that goes to persons who do not work grew far more swiftly, by 970 percent in the case of retirees collecting Social Security checks.

These were workers grown old, or disabled, collecting from a system into which they had paid during their working years. But there was another body of nonworkers, who had never worked, or at least never worked under Social Security covered employment. Their income went up by 851 percent.

If workers were demanding more than they were worth, as some critics said, they were nevertheless being outclassed in this respect by the nonworkers.

Then, maybe the corporations were the culprits.

Michael ran them out into the lineup and reviewed the record of their performance.

Their earnings had grown 458 percent during the 20-year period, a bit faster than wages and salaries paid to workers. However, the owners of the corporation—the stockholders—did not do as well as the employees. The corporate dividends paid grew at a lesser pace, 332 percent.

That turned out to be almost exactly the rate of inflation, meaning that in terms of real buying power, the dividends were almost unchanged.

The difference between what the corporations earned and paid out to stockholders went back into the business, either to upgrade plants or to provide more working capital.

The level of retained earnings went up from $13 billion in 1960 to $91.4 billion in 1980, a growth rate of 600 percent.

That may not have been enough to keep the Japanese or other competitive industrial societies from upgrading their plants faster than U.S. industry.

But it was significantly higher than the growth in personal savings, which grew by 405 percent, against a depreciation rate of 524 percent.

Michael said this difference between personal savings, which provide the capital for long-term investments, and capital consumption, is obviously critical. The "gap" grew from $20 billion in 1960 to $186 billion in 1980, increasing at the rate of 830 percent.

Perhaps the most disturbing trend that showed up in the Tech review was that concerning the business proprietorship.

The man or woman who owns a private business occupies a special role in the American legend. Millions of individuals who work for wages or salaries—even corporate executives—may aspire to join this group.

Because these are the entrepreneurs, the individuals who start new enterprises and are credited as a group with more innovation, and more job creation than any other segment, they are often held up as the model of the free enterprise system.

During the two past decades, the personal income of the proprietors grew by 143 percent. But that was less than half the rate of inflation. If the figures are deflated to dollars of constant value, this segment of the economy lost 13 percent of its earning power during that period.

There is one other suspect often mentioned when the discussion turns to what happened to the American economy — the defense establishment.

The United States as a matter of policy has provided a defense "umbrella" for the free world. The nations which compete with Uncle Sam for industrial markets devote a much smaller share of their gross national product to defense as a result.

Federal expenditures on defense rose from $45.2 billion in 1960 to $136.1 billion in 1980, an increase of 201 percent in unadjusted dollars. But the real increase was but 8 percent, when the expenditure was adjusted for inflation.

And that component of federal spending grew far less swiftly than income maintenance (welfare), up 851 percent; retirement benefits, up 970 percent; or interest on the national debt, up 661 percent.

So, whose fingerprints are on the knife?

The "whodunit" study of the demise of American prosperity by Michael in the role of a computer-equipped Sherlock Holmes tends more to exonerate some suspected likely felons than to fix specific blame.

"Someone suggested it is not a case of murder at all," he said, "but more a case of negligent suicide. That may be as good an explanation as we can get."

Observations and questions

1) The organizing principle of this column is the murder mystery, the "whodunit." The writer asks the economic question. "Who did Uncle Sam in?" All the information in the column relates to that question. Notice, for example, that the first eight sentences are questions? Given this pattern, are you disappointed to discover that there is no clear answer, no economic equivalent to "The butler did it"?

2) Dodson writes that "The man or woman who owns a private business occupies a special role in the American legend." The column implies that the country is suffering because the dream of economic independence and prosperity is no longer a reality for many small business people. Would you have liked to see the author explore this theme in greater detail?

3) The writer uses 25 different statistics in the column. Reread them and see if you can understand their significance. A writer can make use of analogy, comparison, context and pacing to help a reader absorb statistical information. Graphics can also help. Are there instances in which the writer could have helped the reader make better sense of these numbers?

4) Rewrite the following sentence for clarity and brevity and completeness:
   "But it was significantly higher than the growth in personal savings, which grew by 405 percent, against a depreciation rate of 524 percent."

The invisible hand of Adam Smith

APRIL 18, 1982

The man who may have been the founder of economics was hanging around the newspaper racks at Shreve Memorial Library, looking quite spry and cheerful in view of the downbeat economic headlines, not to speak of the fact that he had been dead for the better part of two centuries.

"As I live and breathe," I began, "can it be the original Adam Smith?"

"In spirit and truth," said the somewhat ghostly presence. "As for living and breathing, let's not speak of passing fads."

I felt an embarrassment. Though no one could dismiss his classic work of 1776, the *Wealth of Nations,* as a passing fad, I had just come from the second floor nonfiction stacks. His book was still looking very well preserved, as if nobody had picked it up since, say, the Eisenhower years.

"I'm somewhat familiar with your economic theories," I said. "I bought a copy of your book for a dollar back in the 1940s."

"I might suggest in all humility there have been those in your country who invested their lives in its teaching," he observed. "In a way, all the best of what you have results from that. Still," he said, "a dollar was something in 1947, though not what it had been, of course."

"There's a lot of talk about the money supply these days," I said.

"Balderdash!"

The old eyes were piercing in their intensity. I thought him uncommonly agitated, especially for a ghostly presence.

"Balderdash?"

"Exactly. I spoke quite plainly to that. Let me see. Ah, yes . . . I said that any increase in the quantity of money, while the quantity of commodities circulated by means of it remain the same, could have no other effect than to diminish the value of the money.

"If the nation is to prosper, you need more goods, not more money," he said.

"We seem to have goods," I suggested, "but nobody can buy them."

"Oh, no. The revenue of every society is always precisely equal to the exchangeable value of the whole annual produce of its industry."

"But they tell me," I broke in, waving a hand at the rack of newspapers, "that for lack of money nobody is buying the cars they are making in Detroit, and homebuilding has just about stopped and unemployment is getting worse."

"Even though the capital may be expressed in the same quantity of money," Smith persisted, "the quantity of labor which it could maintain and employ would be increased, and consequently the demand for labor.

"Wages would naturally rise with the demand, and yet might appear to shrink. They might be paid with a smaller quantity of money, but that smaller quantity might purchase a greater quantity of goods."

"I think I see that," I said. "But, nevertheless, there is great concern about money. The Congress...."

"Oh," said Smith. "It tries to do good. I have never known much good done by those who affected to trade for the public good.

"In the latter age of the Republic of Rome, the standard (copper) coin was reduced to the twenty-fourth part of its original value, and instead of weighing a pound, came to weigh only half an ounce."

"I thought it was the decline of morality that did the Romans in. That, and the bloodthirsty barbarians. You mean it was the government, trying to keep people happy?"

"By my time, the English pound contained only a third, the Scots pound about a thirty-sixth, and the French pound about a sixty-fourth part of their original value. A blind man could see why."

"Why?" I asked, rubbing at my eyes.

"The princes and sovereign states...(were then able)...to pay their debts with a smaller quantity of silver than would otherwise have been requisite," he answered.

"Requisite?" I asked.

"Try 'required'...," he said. "Their creditors were really defrauded of a part of what was due them. And all other debtors in the state were allowed the same privilege, and might pay with the same nominal sum of the new and debased coin whatever they had borrowed in the old."

"So that drove up the interest rates?" I asked.

"These operations have always proved favorable to the debtor, and ruinous to the creditor, and have sometimes produced a greater and more universal revolution in the fortunes of private persons, than could have been occasioned by a very great public calamity." he said.

"I think I get your drift," I said somewhat uncertainly. "There are some pretty calamitous things looming around. But the Congress...."

"Maybe plain English is too complicated for you to dig," Smith said, slipping into a vernacular I knew for a fact was not coming from his classic book. "I'm not sure you get my drift at all. Congress is, and ever was, one of the most calamitous things looming. In the words of your current president in a somewhat different context, I think they should butt out."

"And leave it to the Federal Reserve?"

"It would be just as well if they'd butt out too."

"Then who...?"

"Who would control the marketplace? If you remembered what you read in my book, you wouldn't even ask."

"You mean...?"

"Precisely. The invisible hand."

"I thought that was your idea! But I couldn't find a reference in the index," I said. "Maybe it was because I thought you said *unseen* hand."

"Part of my best stuff," he responded. "Here's how it goes: 'As every individual endeavours as much as he can both to employ his capital in the support of domestic industry, and so to direct that industry that its produce may be of the greatest value; every individual necessarily labours to render the annual revenue of the society as great as he can....' "

"That's it!" I broke in. "I recognize that!"

"He neither intends to promote the public interest, nor knows how much he is promoting it... He is in this, as in many cases, led by an invisible hand...."

"You've hit it right on the nose!" I interrupted excitedly. "The invisible hand!"

"He is led by an invisible hand," Smith continued, unperturbed, "to promote an end which was no part of his intention. Nor is it always worse for society that it was no part of it. By pursuing his own interest he frequently promotes that of the society more effectually than when he really intends to promote it...."

I was dazzled. "It's pure *laissez-faire!*"

"That has the sound of French," said Smith. "I prefer my own formulation."

"They tell me we had that, back in the '20s. Then the stock market crashed and brought on the Great Depression," I said.

"If one man be rich, and ride in a carriage, and the other poor, and go afoot, it is not because one rides in the carriage that he is rich and the other poor because he goes afoot. Rather it is because one is rich that he rides in a carriage and the other goes afoot because he is poor," he said.

"I'm not sure what you are saying."

"Let me change the metaphor. I observe that nobody goes afoot in these parts. Do you know dogs? Well, it is not because his tail wags that the dog is content. He wags his tail when he is content. It does not make him content to wag his tail."

"I'm still not getting it," I said.

"It was not the stock market crash that caused the Great Depression. The stock market crash was the tail wagging, or more precisely, the tail ceasing to wag."

"Oh. Then what did cause the Great Depression?" I asked.

"The same thing that will cause the next one, of course," he said.

"And that is?"

"Meddling with the natural order of things. The marketplace is always in the process of correcting itself, and will do so perfectly if there is no artificial interference.

"By the time an observer determines there is something that needs correction, the correction is already in process and by the time an outside correction is applied, the circumstances have already changed so that the problem addressed is not the problem that exists," he said.

"I'm not sure I saw that in your book, in so many words."

"You can infer it, certainly," he said. "My memory is not always precise as to terminology. Except for the really outstanding stuff."

"That sounds pretty vital," I said.

"Of course, vital. But not so outstanding. In fact, I'm not sure I wrote that. Maybe I just thought of it."

"Well, anyway, you're suggesting that the thing for Congress to do, and the Fed, and even the president, who seems to be in your camp, is to go fishing and let things work out?"

"Or, maybe, read a good book," he said.

"Because, as of course, you said so poetically, 'In the end we are all dead....'

"Oh dear me!" said Smith. "I never said any such thing. That was that upstart, Lord Keynes."

"Oh, yes. A different book. But it's hard to keep things straight. They say that economics, no offense, is the dismal science, you know."

"Oh, I quite agree," he said. "Dear me, I was never an economist. I was—am—a philosopher,

an observer and chronicler of simple truths. As
for economists, they've never made much sense
to me. Perhaps dismal is the word."

It seemed an odd way for the talk to end. But
that was it, and the original Adam Smith faded
away, as if manipulated by an invisible hand.

Observations and questions

1) The writer admits to being an admirer of Adam Smith, an advocate of a free market and a limited government, and a political conservative. Which passages in these columns most clearly reflect Dodson's political philosophy?

2) Dodson uses some passages directly from *The Wealth of Nations* and, for the sake of the narrative, puts other words in Adam Smith's mouth. Does the writer supply adequate cues to the reader to make it clear when he is playfully fiddling with history?

3) The naive narrator is a literary technique that goes back at least as far as Chaucer. Can you think of any other literary examples? How does Dodson use the naive narrator in his conversation with Adam Smith? How does the reader react to such a narrator?

4) Adam Smith's language is more difficult to understand than Orland Dodson's. This column would be hard to read if it contained only long passages of 18th century economic theory. Examine the way that Dodson breaks up these passages, spicing the column with fictional dialogue and narration.

5) Humor makes the economic philosophy in this column palatable. The writer derives humor from at least three sources:

   A) The contrast of archaic language and modern slang, *balderdash* vs. *dig.*

   B) Jokes about death: "As for living and breathing, let's not speak of passing fads."

C) The dramatic scene of Adam Smith making a ghostly appearance to a business writer in Shreveport, Louisiana.

Discuss the effectiveness of these techniques.

The three great numbers and what they mean

MARCH 14, 1982

Public confidence in the economy bobs up and down, like a boat tied short to the dock, with the ebb and flow of three great numbers which constitute the tide of the marketplace—the Gross National Product (GNP), the Unemployment Rate, and the Money Supply.

The tides are real. But the numbers are illusions.

Take GNP, which Webster's Dictionary and the Associated Press, as reason would dictate, assume to mean the sum of goods and services produced in the nation.

It's not so.

The Gross National Product is a composite, not of what is produced, but what is consumed. Its five components are consumer spending, government spending, fixed investments, net exports and the change in inventories.

You mine 16 tons of coal and call up the Bureau of Economic Analysis and tell them you've got something to add to the GNP and they'll laugh at you.

When somebody buys and burns the coal, it counts as production.

Scout's honor.

A Massachusetts statistician, Leonard H. Lempert, explains GNP this way:

In a given city, households use 40 million gallons of water (consumer spending), the municipality uses 5 million gallons (government spending), private firms buy 10 million to fill reflecting pools for air conditioning (fixed investment), the reservoir rises 3 million gallons (change in inventory) and 2 million gallons escapes over the spillway (net exports).

The total is 60 million gallons. But none of the activities produced a drop of water. But that

60 million gallons is the water production, if you
figure it as the GNP is worked out.

None of this is news to the experts who come
up with the GNP numbers, but they take the
number very seriously nevertheless. The GNP
is the key determinant of whether the country
is in a recession. When it turns down for two suc-
cessive quarters, the recession is on, officially.
And it won't be over, officially, until the GNP
is clearly turning up.

Countless individual business decisions are
made on the basis of what the GNP is indicating,
by people who do not know how the figure is
worked out.

For all the importance attached to the GNP,
it is updated by quarters, so the public is buffered
from worrying about it every day, or even every
month.

Not so with the money supply.

The money supply figures come out every
week. Financiers, stock brokers and people con-
cerned about interest rates await their appearance with bated breath.

Since the pursuit of money is what keeps people working and scheming and planning and worrying, then of course things look better the higher
the supply. Right? And the more there is, the
more to lend, so interest rates come down?

Wrong.

The money supply goes up when everybody
who can find a co-signer borrows to the hilt at
the bank.

If the supply goes up, the stock market turns
down. As interest goes up, investors find it more
attractive to lend money than to take the risk
of investing.

If money supply goes down, interest rates
drop, and stocks are more attractive to investors.
So the market goes up.

What matters is not how much money there
really is, or how it was earned, or even whether
the person who has it earned it or borrowed it
at outrageous interest. What matters is how
much has been borrowed.

Thus the higher the supply, the less there is around.

If I'm lying I'm dying.

There was jubilation among bankers and economists late in February when the Federal Reserve reported a drop of $3.1 billion in the money supply. The *New York Times* described the mood in the credit markets as "ebullient."

Why?

A financial economist at Paine Webber found it reassuring that the economy was slowing down: "By the end of March, a weak economy will generate a weaker demand for money.... The money supply is finally heading in the right direction," said Maurey Harris, the economist.

The third Great Number deals with employment. Each month the Department of Labor counts the number of people at work, and the number looking for work, and comes up with the unemployment rate, expressed as a percentage. Everybody takes that very seriously, because things are really serious when a capable, willing worker can't get a job.

But is the number real? Does it reflect a hard count?

Not quite. Consider this: the *Times* publishes a chart, monthly on this page, so readers can compare the current level of employment in the Shreveport metropolitan area to what it was one year before, or in any intervening month.

Each month, as the Department of Labor sends its monthly report, the chart is updated by placing a dot on the scale to show total employment. The idea is the reader can compare where the dot was on the scale last month, or last year, and tell whether there are more or fewer people working.

Last week, the Department of Labor sent in the figures for January. The department said there was a loss of about 2,000 jobs from December to January.

But the new number representing people at work was 8,000 higher than indicated by the

December dot on the *Times* chart.

It caused the *Times* serious concern. How had its chart gotten so far off base?

Not to worry, an official of the Department of Labor counseled. Only the benchmark had changed.

The statistician chuckled. "I guess you didn't notice we changed the benchmark."

The benchmark?

"It changes every year, in March," he said.

And the result was 7,000 people, give or take a few, just popped up in their figures. They were not people as you may know them, like those who moved in from Waskom or Plain Dealing or Des Moines to join the Shreveport labor force.

Obviously, people are assumed to be here, who were not assumed to have been here last year, or even last month.

Employers spend eleventy-jillion dollars a year preparing and sending in forms to the government showing how many people they have on the payroll.

But that's not where the Department of Labor gets its figures.

Instead it hires the Census Bureau to make regular surveys of population samples and to ask the people if they consider themselves employed or unemployed.

And then the percentage is multiplied by the number of samples that size, which there would be in the population. The result of that is the figure they publish. Except, first they go through a 70-step procedure.

There are defenders with somewhat rational explanations for all these methods. People who make big decisions on the basis of what those figures show are usually interested in long-term trends, not the data for today, and they understand how the data are gathered in any case.

Ordinary mortals, who know perfectly well that the banker is not going to be satisfied with an "estimated" checking account balance or an "approximate" payment on the bank note, perhaps ought not take the GNP, unemployment and money supply figures too much to heart.

Dr. Don Wilcox, dean of business at LSU-Shreveport, and Dr. Phillip Fincher, who teaches banking and economics at Louisiana Tech, agreed that the figures are based on estimates, that they are not precisely what they purport to be, but that they do provide useful and reliable guides to long-term trends.

But too much attention to them by the public, Dr. Wilcox suggested, tends to bring about marketplace decisions which "reinforce" the apparent trends, and thus could make bad news worse or good news better.

Besides, Dr. Fincher said, the dominant school of economists tends to believe that it takes from six months to two years for a significant change in the money supply, for example, to translate into action in the real marketplace.

By the time it helps or hurts, you'll be hearing other numbers anyway.

Observations and questions

1) Often a good lead defines in miniature the structure of the whole story. Notice how Dodson's straightforward lead on the "three great numbers" tips off the reader on how the column will be organized.

2) Writers often pace a story, especially a complicated one, so that readers can "catch up" with the information. Dodson uses short sentences to slow the reader down. Notice how he controls the pace of the information by using sentence length and even fragments: "Not so with the money supply."

3) At times, Dodson's language seems homey and familiar. Discuss the effects of the following phrases: *Scout's honor; If I'm lying I'm dying; Waskom or Plain Dealing; eleventy-jillion.* Do they seem out of place in a fairly technical economic story?

4) Examine the ways in which the writer makes use of outside experts throughout his work. What roles do these authorities play in Dodson's column?

5) The use of analogy can often help a writer explain a complicated, abstract issue. Examine carefully Leonard Lempert's analogy comparing the GNP to a city's water supply. In what ways does it inform the reader?

6) The Gross National Product is often described in newspapers as "the sum of goods and services produced in the nation." Having read Dodson's column, would you feel comfortable using this definition in your newspaper?

Orland Dodson at work

Oil drilling was drying up, neither homes nor cars were selling well, merchants were just hanging on, and the national news was filled with portents of economic disaster. There could hardly have been a better time for Shreveporters to hear about an increase of 8,000 in the number of men and women at work in the metropolitan area.

That news came in the monthly report from the Louisiana Department of Labor. But unaccountably, it was included in the same report that said the unemployment rate was up, and that there were 2,000 fewer jobs!

Obviously one of the figures was wrong. How could there be 2,000 fewer jobs, AND 8,000 more people holding jobs?

The mystery deepened when we tried to update a chart run each month on the Sunday business section front. The department reported that there had been thousands more people at work a month ago, and a year ago, than our chart had shown.

I called the statistician at the local office of the Department of Labor. He chuckled.

"I guess you didn't notice we changed the benchmark," he said.

His explanation of the benchmark, which it turns out the department adjusts each year to reflect supposed population growth and other factors, led to more questions, which I posed to the local office and to higher-ups in the state capital.

The answers added up to a plain conclusion. Not one hard figure was in the report. All were educated guesses worked up from spot checks with certain key employers, random samplings by the Bureau of the Census, and intuitive assumptions.

The explanations were so well phrased, and delivered so calmly, it occurred to me for a moment to suppose that everybody but me had known all along that the figures were cooked up as a standard routine. But when I bounced the idea off some of my friends outside the news business, they were as shocked as I. One of them raised another question:

If the employment figures were fiction, what numbers could we believe?

It occurred to me that I had seen something recently in an out-of-town paper that had caused me to wonder if I really understood the money supply. Back at the office, I searched until I found it. It was the *New York Times* report on Wall Street reaction to an announcement by the Federal Reserve the previous afternoon that the money supply had declined by several billion dollars. The reaction was jubilation, causing me to wonder why it was good news that there was less money around.

I called on the local experts—a senior vice president at a major local bank and professors of economics at local universities. The explanation was ingenious, and unanimous. The money supply figure really reflects the level of borrowings. Thus the more money owed, the larger the supply, and the banks get more picky about the quality of loans they approve. Therefore, the more there is the less there is, and the higher the interest borrowers must pay. And the less there is, the more there is, and the less it costs to borrow some.

That sounded so marvelous to me that I was bold enough to ask about the "number of numbers," the Gross National Product. I had seen it defined dozens of times in the wire reports as the sum of goods and services produced in the nation. But I was on a roll, delirious with joy. Was it possible the GNP is also a hoax?

I asked one of the economics professors for the components of the GNP. He gave me four off the top of his head and looked up the other one. Consumer spending. Government spending. Fixed investments. Net exports. And oh, yes, the change in inventories.

It was uncanny. At least three of the five sounded like consumption instead of production. I pressed him about that.

"Well, yes," he said. "Of course you can't consume until you produce." Then he cited an explanation by a statistician comparing the five components to changes in the water level in a municipal reservoir.

This example made no mention of rainfall, which is where we get all the water that I know about in reservoirs.

Incredibly, I had a shutout going. I had authoritative testimony that all three of the "great numbers" were illusions.

But there was a problem. None of the experts wanted to be identified directly with what was shaping up as an attack on procedures they use routinely in their work, and which they feel are sufficiently analogous to reality to serve their purposes.

I want to be sensitive to such concerns. These are people upon whom I must depend frequently for help in doing my work. So I cannot afford to drag them, kicking and screaming, onto the stage to be embarrassed.

That meant I would have to do the main dance myself, practically solo. And all I had for the overture were the somewhat sticky explanation of how the employment figures are only estimates, the water supply analogy to the GNP, and the clip from the *New York Times* including a brief quote from a Wall Street analyst about how nice it is that the money supply has dropped.

The direct sources from my own research had to be brought on after the main action, lending credence to the whole dance with the assurance, obligatory if I used them at all, that even if the figures are not exactly what they seem to pretend to be, that is not why the sky is falling.

So, I let them have the last word. But first I wanted to get it all laid out for the readers that those dreary figures that slap them in the face when they open the newspaper or turn on a newscast are, strictly speaking, concocted of horsefeathers and moonbeams.

The readers I heard from indicated they got the message.

A conversation with
Orland Dodson

CLARK: I notice in your biography that you've switched back and forth from broadcast to print. Do you have any sense of how that might have affected your writing?

DODSON: I think I tend to write more for the ear than people who have worked only in print. I can tell you a story that goes way back. I was working in Galveston as a radio reporter, and as was typical in those days, I was the whole news staff. So I had to cover the whole waterfront, so to speak. At the same time I was the Galveston correspondent for the *Houston Post.*

I developed a system whereby I would write the material for the newscast with a dateline on it, so that I could send a carbon to the *Post* by Western Union. So in a way, I was trying to do two things. Everybody told me that you have to write differently for broadcast than you do for print, but I suppose I developed some kind of an alloy, a hybrid. And I suppose that had an effect on the way I write.

I see in your writing what English teachers call *voice,* the illusion that the writer is speaking directly to the reader.

That makes sense to me. I'm sometimes accused of writing for people who move their lips when they read.

You are the first person to win a business writing award from ASNE. The category was added because of the increasing importance of business and economic writing in newspapers. What do you think of that?

We started the business desk here about three years ago. I have been astounded at the response. It's almost like we were pouring water in the desert. The business community had been accustomed to feeling that if they wanted something said in the newspaper, they had to buy the space or write a letter to the editor. They've been very supportive, and we just get a flood of personal items and new business openings. I've been really pleased and surprised at the people not directly involved in a business who seem interested in the broader economic questions.

I'm usually not interested in the writing on most business pages. It seems to be special interest writing which excludes me as a reader. Yet when I read your work I had a different feel. You were writing for a general audience of educated readers rather than for business types.

I'd like to think I'm writing for more than just people who are running stores and businesses. But I want to say this about the business field. I sort of fell into journalism because it beat working on the farm. The common perception in those days of business writers was that they wrote what was called the BOM. In the old days, it meant Business Office Must. When one of those came down, it meant that the publisher had instructed someone in the news department to do a little puff piece on so and so. That didn't do anything to endear the people in the business community to the newsroom.

As journalists, we get very interested in politicians and pressure groups, but the business guys in those days would lean on the advertising department and get a BOM.

But I found out that what people do in business is to my way of thinking more daring and courageous day by day than being in politics. The first time I realized what courage it might take to be in business was many years ago when

I was working at the little paper in Pasadena (Texas). I got to know some of the people downtown who were in business, little retail stores, and I would have coffee with them once in a while.

I was talking to a guy who had a little men's clothing store. He was explaining to me what he had to do to keep in reasonably good shape with the bank and with his suppliers. He had a problem with cash flow. He had to pay his bill by the 10th of the month to get a discount of 2 percent from his supplier. Sometimes he just didn't have the money in the bank, and he knew he wouldn't have it in the bank for five or six days. So once in a while he would write a check, but wouldn't sign it, and send it in. As long as he didn't do that too often, they would just drop him a line, send him back the check, and say, "You forgot to sign it." And he'd buy two or three days of time that way and get his discount.

I said, "Boy, that is really daring."

This may sound contrary to that story, but I think by and large business relationships are conducted on a very high level of honor. When you get to the bottom line, a guy who stays in business for a long time is able to do so only because he is able to deal with his suppliers and his landlord and his bankers. He makes his reputation as the sort of guy who keeps his word, or who doesn't keep his word.

You don't sound as if you assume an adversarial posture toward those things and people that you write about.

That's correct. That doesn't mean that if somebody does something crooked in business and gets caught at it, that I would be hesitant about writing about it. I'm not suggesting that all guys in business wear white hats, but I am suggesting that they do play an interesting game. What they do is as exciting to me as watching a baseball game.

**Do you try to convey that sense of excite-
ment to your readers? Do you try to write
about business the way you've described it?**

I'd like to think I'm trying to work towards that
end. I don't think I can write about business and
make it seem as interesting as baseball, no. But
I'd like to think of that as kind of a goal.

**The stories in this collection seem more
about economics than business. But I am interested in other types of stories that you do
routinely.**

When I've found a businessman who has done
the Horatio Alger story, that really turns me on.
And surprisingly, you can find those guys. We
have a section of town called Agars. There are
four or five sizable industrial employers up there.
But there are hundreds of small businesses that
support the oil and gas industry. That's the kind
of place where a guy can go into business in a
little store front with a welding tool, and if he's
good at what he does, and prompt in making his
deliveries and keeps his promises, he can build
a business over time.

    I wrote about one of those guys. He was just
a merchant. He went into the nut and bolt
business, selling fasteners. He starts out with a
little line like you'd find in the neighborhood
hardware store. By the time I heard about him,
he had built a factory. He was making nuts and
bolts, and some of them were huge. He'd make
a nut and a bolt, a dozen of which would make
a truckload.

Wow, what would you use those for?

That's the question I asked. Who owns a boat
that big? And what does he do with it? The ones
he showed me were being purchased by a con-
tractor with the Department of Defense to put
propellers on Navy submarines. It had taken him

25 years to build his business. He had reached
the point where he had achieved national stature
because he just digs nuts and bolts.

**I'd like to ask you about these columns
because in a way they are very different
from the stories you've just described, and
I would think they would be harder to write.**

Once in a while I get the idea that I'm the only
guy in the country who doubts things like the
economic numbers. But I talk to business people
and they tell me: "Well, listen. I see by the papers
that things are really tough, but I'm just doing
great." I remember a restaurant operator who
told me that in the last recession. I stopped in
and asked, "How's business?" He said, "This is
the finest recession I've ever been in! If we have
recessions like this every year, I'm going to get
rich."

From that type of experience, you try to
figure what the hell is really happening in the
country. And does anyone really know?

**It seems to me that you try to set a leisurely
pace for your readers. All the hard
information isn't packed into long
paragraphs.**

I identify with that. If we're going to get an
audience—not just people who understand
figures—you have to pace it. I realize there's
nothing harder to read than a statistical table.
It can put you to sleep in a heck of a hurry. Yet
some of that stuff is important. I try to be
lighthearted about it. You have to pace it. You
have to get an anecdote in there to illustrate
what you're talking about. Or at least an
example.

**Would your columns be more readable, and
easier to write, if they were accompanied by
informational graphics?**

We're doing more of that now. We're a Gannett paper and *USA Today* uses a lot of that stuff. A lot of it looks really good.

You express both belief in the American system and yet some skepticism about the economic numbers. Are those contradictory feelings? Do you ever say: Is anyone in control here?

My favorite philosopher is Adam Smith. And what Adam Smith said about the market was if the government would just keep its cotton pickin' hands off, the market would solve its problem. My impression is that we need a cop in the marketplace to keep the thieves out and make sure the scales are accurate. Smith also said that whenever two or three businessmen get together, for whatever purpose, sooner or later the question will get around to how will we get prices up. What I distrust is an alliance between business and government. Yet it's very tempting.

Isn't it rather nostalgic to admire Adam Smith? Did Adam Smith ever envision Gannett, or AT&T, or multi-national corporations?

I'm sure he didn't. Interestingly enough, his book was published the same year we started the revolution, 1776. I guess I relate to that era. I like what they did in 1776 (laughter) and I like what he said. Sometimes I think the one is as important as the other. What Smith had to say about the free market was almost as influential in setting the policies of the U.S. in its early days as the Declaration of Independence.

So you consider yourself a political conservative. I just want you to go on the record.

Oh, yes. Except I'm so old, let me get this on the record, that I used to define myself as a Jefferson Liberal. There are four or five guys like me in the world. We would say that we're the real liberals because our concept of the liberal notion is a small government that does exactly what the Constitution says it should do, and doesn't bug me about anything else.

Do you write quickly?

Yes, I think I do. The physical act of getting it in the computer, yes.

Do you rewrite much?

Sometimes I rewrite over and over again and sometimes I rewrite very lightly. It depends on whether it makes sense to me when I read it.

What would cause you to rewrite something?

Outside of checking it to see I've got the right quote and the right figures, which is the most important thing, then I want to know, "Does it sound good to me? Does it seem to me to flow?" If I find it doesn't flow, I might cut out some stuff because that's probably the reason it doesn't flow. I stopped to dwell too long on something that doesn't need that much attention.

I'm trying to be honest with you. Some of this stuff is complicated, and not too easily understood; I certainly don't understand everything myself. Sometimes I'm trying to explain something. I read it and it doesn't make sense to me. I'm going to be better off, and the reader's going to be better off, if I don't pretend to try to explain that. I just get it out of there because I'm just going to compound the confusion.

Where do your story ideas come from?

I try to do two things consistently. I try to read almost everything that comes across the desk.

There's just a mass of it. Press releases and corporate reports. I throw away most of the material. But if something strikes me as interesting, I might tuck that in my pocket and next time I'm out on the street, I might ask a banker, "What do you think of this? Does this make sense to you?" And the other thing I do is to try to spend as much time as I can out of the office just talking to people in business. The most remarkable thing about journalism to me is this: No matter what I go out to get, if I set out with a plan in mind, I'm going to get a story. It may not be the story I set out to get. The more you go out, the more people you talk to, the more story ideas you have. And I can sit here at my desk and scratch my head and cudgel my brain and think and think and I won't come out with as nearly as good an idea as I'll find in an hour or two downtown.

How do you organize the material you collect for a story. Do you have any system you work by?

I really don't. I try to stack up the material more or less in the order I intend to address it. But I try to be familiar enough with it so that when I have an idea for a lead—a notion of how I'll get started—I start writing. As much as I can, I try writing without going back to the notes. Then after I finish, or when I just get stuck, I'll go to the notes. I operate under the assumption that by the time I get to the keyboard, I know what I'm going to say.

Each of your stories has an interesting focus, a center of gravity, that enables you to write a unified, well-developed piece. The "They" story, for example.

I know how that came about. I kept walking around town talking to people about their problems and everybody kept saying, "It's going to be OK as soon as 'they' bring interest rates down." When I talked to businessmen on the street or guys who have stores, I thought they were talking about the bankers. But the bankers were saying the same thing. Maybe they were talking about Paul Volcker and the Federal Reserve. But they kept saying "they." That's when I came up with the concept that "they" is no one group of people. That everyone is a "they," if they've got money stashed in the bank. And "they" are delighted to take the interest.

You use experts and academic authorities in many of your stories.

There's a gentleman down at Louisiana Tech, about 75 miles down the road. Dr. James Robert Michael just loves numbers. He has all this census and Bureau of Economic Analysis material available to him. He loves nothing better than to get into those computers and see just how many numbers he can churn out. He and I quite often talk about these things. He'll see something he thinks is interesting, and he'll call me about it. He'll churn out page after page of tables. He'll turn flips if I ask him a question and come out with a huge mass of material. He's a very valuable ally for me and a fine resource and I work him a lot. I know there's a story in there, but I've got to find where it is.

Manuela Hoelterhoff
Finalist, Commentary

MANUELA HOELTERHOFF joined the editorial page staff of the *Wall Street Journal* in 1975. She serves as arts editor, writing about opera, painting, architecture and other topics. She was born in Hamburg, West Germany, in 1949. She attended Hofstra University on Long Island and the Institute of Fine Arts of New York University. Before joining the *Journal*, she served as arts editor of the *Academic Encyclopedia*, editor of *Art & Auction* magazine, and associate editor of *Portfolio* magazine. She is the winner of this year's Pulitzer Prize for criticism.

7,000 rocks and the state of contemporary art

SEPTEMBER 17, 1982

Illustrious writers and artists, among them Goethe, once praised this city's prettiness and convivial mood. That was long before a few hours of bombing in 1943 melted away Kassel's medieval past. The new Kassel rose like a crow out of the ashes, a sad patchwork of auto routes and modern buildings that look all the more sullen in the grey weather typical this time of year. Now few who come to Kassel praise it.

But every four or five years, an immense number of people *do* come here, attracted by "documenta," an art exhibition of extraordinary size, cost and (usually) controversy. No other show of contemporary art can be said to have "documenta's" impact.

The first "documenta" took place in 1955. For Germany, the exhibition was a big event. The focus on international contemporary art emphasized the country's departure from the viciously narrow-minded art policies of the Nazis, and the location was intended to bolster the spirit and ledger of an apathetic city, once centrally located, now depressingly close to the border of Communist East Germany.

Right now Kassel is the scene of the seventh "documenta," and by the time the show ends on Sept. 28, an estimated 370,000 people will have wandered through the three exhibition spaces (the Fridericianum, the Orangerie and the Neue Galerie) and past outdoor pieces placed in the spacious parklands along the Fulda River.

"Documenta's" visitors are expected to enrich Kassel by an estimated $8 million and that probably makes its citizenry a lot happier than some of the art and fun people suddenly plunked down in their sober midst. As I headed into the

Fridericianum—a mighty 18th century structure stuffed with art—I walked past two non-exhibitors completely sprayed with silver paint peddling "astronaut art" and a bizarre man dressed in sandals and black raincoat who drew a huge crowd singing to an imaginary flea he held in a little box. There was also a tremendous pile of rocks on the lawn in front of the museum. More on that in a minute.

What's on view was chosen by Rudi Fuchs, a Dutch curator at a museum in Eindhoven. Working with a small advisory group and a large budget of about $3 million, he selected 1,000 works by 180 artists. So who's out? Who's in? What's new? Hard to say at first glance, though you'd have to be a recent emigre from another planet not to notice two things: Unlike past "documentas," this one plays down new American art in favor of Italian and German contributions, and like all "documentas," the show only barely recognizes the existence of women artists. Yes, the show does include intriguing pieces by Elvira Bach, Jonathan Borofsky and Jenny Holzer, among others. But on the whole, European macho, so evident in politics these days, also undermines Kassel.

The show is oddly arranged. Works by a single artist are often scattered throughout different floors, even different buildings, making individual contributions difficult to assess. There is a two-volume catalog to compensate for skimpy labels. But since it includes works not in the show and bits of text by such people as Pasolini and Barthes who never saw the show because they are dead, you might as well be carrying a street map to Kabul.

The majority of visitors thus wander about bewildered or bemused past a room partly filled with lumber, a twig labyrinth and startling juxtapositions: a heap of crushed metal by John Chamberlain, placed in front of hieroglyphic paintings by A.R. Penck. Members of the press at least had the benefit of a long, dreamy letter

written by Mr. Fuchs to explain the theoretical
underpinnings of his "documenta."

This is the gist of it: Past "documentas" focus-
ed on movements like pop art or individual artists. This one focuses on art works. Art has been
twisted by polemics and corrupted by con-
sumerism. This is deplorable because art is
"pure, quiet and discreet."

One may wonder how on earth Mr. Fuchs or
anyone out of college can seriously entertain such
pristine, world-remote thoughts. Still, the notion
that art is something special is not unappealing
in a time of monster shows and hype. And a hand-
ful of pieces lends some visual support to his
ideas. On view is a tall, thick column covered in
gold leaf by James Lee Byars. Simple in design,
it's also costly and handsome. Nearby is a
mysterious long wall by Greek artist Kounellis
similarly covered with a gold-like substance that
recalls Byzantine icons. The wall is juxtaposed
with a coatstand to symbolize, I suppose, the conflict between eternal art and everyday life. A little simple? Sure. But in material and size, the
work makes quite an impact.

Unfortunately, you don't have to walk much
further to determine that the majority of selec-
tions are more shallow than hallowed. Typical
is a washline of aluminum foil objects which Lu-
ciano Fabro suspended between two walls. It's
called "I Gioielli" (The Jewels) but looks like it
was hammered together by a bunch of blind men
in a junk shop.

The search for a pure art seems to have led
Mr. Fuchs to favor artists working in the
minimal or conceptual modes prevalent in the
late '60s and '70s. As a result, half-finished
thoughts, painfully birthed by tiny talents with
no great technical skills, are celebrated for their
reductive abilities and "honesty." And that
means that this "documenta" neither documents
the immediate past nor charts (let's hope) the
course of art in the near future.

Even Robert Mapplethorpe's or Cindy Sher-
man's powerful photographs, for example, can't

reveal the vast achievements in this field.
There's no hint of Pattern and Decoration and
the selection of Neo-Expressionists is peculiar
(the absence of Julian Schnabel seems malicious).
Video art is represented by two hypnotizing
pieces by Dara Biernbaum, but that's it. Realism
is virtually ignored. There are few sculptures in
the park and most of those have been destroyed
or covered with graffiti by visitors who, perhaps
because the materials used often look like refuse,
treat the pieces as such. And so, at a time when
many of us thought art was getting more
pluralistic, we're once again marched past a canvas titled "Impact of Brush No. 50" and Carl Andre's rusting, steel-plated walkways.

Which brings me to the talk of the town: the
huge assortment of 7,000 basalt rocks outside the
Fridericianum. They were deposited there at the
request of Joseph Beuys, Germany's interna-
tionally acclaimed burgher-baiter. Mr. Beuys
usually works with lard and felt, creating pieces
that can be revoltingly fascinating. But he also
plans happenings with left-wing sociopolitical
overtones and poor Kassel is still shaking its com-
munal head over his latest escapade.

Using the slogan "more trees not
bureaucratese," he set up a little stand by the
basalt outcropping to sell oak trees. Each tree
sale reduces the pile by one. The tree is then
carted off to its destination together with the rock
to symbolize (this I had to be told) living nature
conquering unyielding government.

"Baffling," said one old woman to another as
they wandered through the square. "We've
already got so many." And in truth, Kassel is
very rich in beautifully maintained parklands
with plenty of trees. Understandably, the project
is considered risible. "Better girls than Beuys"
says a much-seen graffito. And a few trees
planted near a hotel were murdered by acid-
pouring pranksters.

Much greater favor is extended to a giant
pickax placed by Claes Oldenburg on the bank

of the Fulda River. Unlike Beuys's absurdity, it relates to Kassel in an intelligent and amusing way. Overlooking Kassel is a park with a castle and an elaborate waterfall dominated by a gigantic figure of Hercules. And a new myth says that Zeus's son, not Claes, sent the pick sailing through the air to its present location. Would that more pieces had this impact and connective tissue with the real world.

In fact, the piece that ultimately lingers in my mind was an uncatalogued, spontaneous creation I discovered going down a staircase at the Fridericianum. No doubt inspired by the show's prevalent summer semester workshop look, three visitors had fashioned a heartfelt, three-dimensional *billet doux* and left it on a windowsill. The assemblage comprised a soda can, an artfully folded napkin, a piece of chewed gum and a wrapper. The label read: Title: Untitled. Year: 1982. By: Iris, Anja and Birgit.

Observations and questions

1) Hoelterhoff writes in a mixed genre. Her piece contains elements of travel writing and of criticism. Read several travel stories and several straight art reviews. Try to discern the demands of each genre. Consider how these elements merge and interact in Hoelterhoff's work.

2) This story contains *narration* and *exposition*. The writer tells a story and derives meaning. Reread her stories with those two categories in mind. Cite instances where her observations become judgments?

3) Analyzing Hoelterhoff's style, speculate on her audience. What educational level, degree of affluence and specialized knowledge does the writer assume?

4) Underline any technical allusions that you don't understand or that are not clear from context. Do you know who Jonathan Borofsky is? Or Carl Andre? Do you understand the "minimal or conceptual modes prevalent in the late 1960s and '70s?" Do these references detract from the piece?

5) Images, metaphors, analogies allow the writer to compare abstract ideas to concrete things. This may be especially helpful to the critic who often finds herself describing the abstruse or impressionistic. Consider the following images and their effects on the reader:
   ...You might as well be carrying a street map to Kabul.
   ...The new Kassel rose like a crow out of the ashes.
   ...looks like it was hammered together by a bunch of blind men in a junk shop.

6) Hoelterhoff uses an interesting technique in discussing the 7,000 basalt rocks. She promises "more on that in a minute." How might a reader react to that phrase?

7) The writer obviously enjoyed the piece of impromptu art she describes in this story's conclusion. How does that ending summarize the writer's opinion of this art festival?

Golden Prague: Travels through a police state

OCTOBER 15, 1982

We still had a kilometer or so to go, but all the welcoming signs were already there: the barbed wire as far as the eye could see; the watchtowers; the closely trimmed meadows that couldn't hide a squadron of relapsed field mice. We pulled up the car in front of a roadblock manned by glum, baby-faced guards carrying machine guns.

We'd driven here from Vienna—less than an hour from the border and some 200 miles from Prague, our destination. Straight ahead was what Neville Chamberlain described as "a faraway little land that few of us know anything about." Chamberlain, to be sure, didn't, and as a result Czechoslovakia became for a few bloody years part of the Nazi empire. Now, of course, thanks to people with similarly informed geopolitical views, the Czechs are tied with cement overshoes to their socialist comrades in the Soviet Union.

Grotesque trials still dispense bent justice to signers of Charter 77. Artist Jiri Kolar has been sentenced in absentia to a one-year prison term for residing in Paris without official Czech permission and writer Vaclav Havel is in jail. Others, like Pavel Kohout and Zdenek Mlynar have been forced into exile for "counter-revolutionary activities," which usually means expressing some doubt that the most terrific kind of socialism is that with a beefy, Stalinist face.

As the contents of my car were being rearranged on the pavement and scrutinized with the attention most normal people give to menus, I kept reassuring myself that I had no reason to be this sweaty and nervous. The sole purpose of my trip was to acquaint myself with a city many deem more beautiful than Vienna. I wanted to walk around, look at art and have a four-day vacation. I harbored no subversive materials. On my person were no names of dissidents who might tell me tales of horror in dimly lit rooms.

About an hour passed. As we wondered whether we should have just checked through to Siberia (also straight ahead and to the right), we were waved on, leaving behind a guard glued to our "not permissible" copy of Der Spiegel. He is now the Warsaw Pact's expert on herpes, that week's cover story.

This entry to Czechoslovakia with its grotesque mix of comedy and fear set the tone for the whole trip. A few days in Prague and it's easy to see why writers like emigre novelist Milan Kundera can only describe life here as a satire, a long-running black comedy of errors constantly being extended, rewritten and refurbished by party hacks on hire from Moscow.

That policeman, for instance. How did he come to pop up so suddenly at the window of my car? We'd pulled to a curb inside Prague to check the address of our hotel. How nice, I thought. He'll point the way. Instead he asked for our passports. Then he demanded 100 crowns (about $10). Then he looked like he was going to shoot us because we couldn't stop laughing. But it was pretty funny: Here we were 10 minutes in Prague and already forced to bribe a bulwark of the socialist order.

Soon we were unpacking at a hotel my invariably inaccurate guidebook praised for its old world charm. The blurb failed to mention the courteous operator who dials all your calls. "The place is better wired than a disco. Every word is taped," said a German journalist friend who took us to an art show in a park outside Prague.

This exhibition was by non-union artists who work in surrealist and abstract styles unacceptable to the cultural ministry. If they can show at all, it is in provincial galleries or virtually inaccessible places like this park.

(They are sometimes allowed, however, to sell works abroad through an export agency that takes a one-third cut. Foreign currency needs transcend ideology.)

In fact, none of the artists care to be described as dissidents, though their subjects—one figurative sculpture has teeth like a trap— reflect some doubt about the human condition. The quality of the work was suprisingly high. But even more fascinating were the people: I could have been in New York's SoHo. An art show like this brings out Prague's fashionable few sporting punk haircuts, T-shirts and chic puffy pants.

I chatted with a few artists, went on several studio visits and intended to spend much of this article discussing their work, praising their spirit. But a few days ago, I received a letter smuggled out via a friend which implored me not to write anything. Any mention of their difficulties would make life even more intolerable.

And so, I must not write anything about the art critic who's been hounded and interrogated ever since she signed Charter 77; the sculptor who keeps his large-scale works in bits and pieces in his small *atelier* waiting for the day he may assemble and show them; the painter who's somehow managed to produce quality work for 15 years while his family has been harassed because of his Western contacts.

I'll write instead about the city that mistreats them. It is beautiful. Prague spreads out gracefully on both sides of the Vltava River (celebrated in Smetana's tone poem,"The Moldau"). Few bombs fell on Prague in World War II and the government lavishes on buildings the kind of affection it fails to bestow on the occupants. In contrast to people, buildings rarely disappear, but are carefully renovated down to the last piece of gold leaf and stucco swagger.

When you walk from Stare Mesto, the oldest part of Prague, across the sculpture-studded

Charles Bridge and up to Hradcany, the castle area that dominates the city, you look out over reddish roofs and pastel-colored buildings that give off an almost Italianate glow. It's easy to see why admirers have called Prague "the golden city."

Within half an hour, you can walk through some 600 years of history. Dating to Prague's early years is a 13th century synagogue and an old Jewish cemetery with some 12,000 toppling tombstones that sprout from the ground like bizarre mushrooms. Nearby is the aptly named Parizska Street with opulent, 19th century facades that would fit in smoothly on the Champs Elysees. The baroque church of St. Nicholas, decorated by the Dienzenhofers, vies with anything I've seen in Bavaria and Vienna. And suddenly you're reminded that Prague was once a *European* city, part of the Austro-Hungarian empire. It's farther west than Vienna. Not until the communist takeover in 1948, was the city's orientation brutally turned eastward.

And after the first aesthetic rush, you get the disturbing feeling that what you're admiring is a neatly maintained, lovely looking comatose patient. Prague is without the bustling people that make cities come alive. There's no pulse here, no heartbeat, only the pallid blip-blip emitted by a planned economy.

People either stand in queues for everything from meat to ice cream cones, or trudge past window displays that would make Marx burst into tears of regret. At night, a lack of illumination and people turns the place into a spooky, de Chirico-like townscape. There are a number of attractive restaurants but they cater almost exclusively to tourists and are considered risky territory for Czechs. Odd how socialist countries turn out asocial people.

Indeed, the gap between past and present-day Prague, reality and propaganda, tourist and citizen, is wide enough to accommodate panzer units of the size that obliterated the Prague spring of 1968 when the country did, very briefly, come alive.

"How do intelligent people keep sane?" I ask a friend of a friend as we sit in a small park away from microphones. "Most of us ignore the discrepancy. It's too much of a mental strain to have your mind run on two tracks all the time," he answers. "And who thinks about politics when you're spending all your spare time scrambling between stores to put something on your back or on the table."

Speculation is one way Czechs try to enhance their sparely appointed lives (bribery— euphemistically called "use of position"—and barter are the other two). Every few minutes someone would come up to me and whisper: "Wechsel? Exchange? Dollars?" What? I thought. Commit a crime against the state in broad daylight on Wenceslas Square? Not on my life. Then a mad-looking fellow carrying a Tennessee Williams book sidled up and said "25 for one." Well, that was better than twice the official rate and we sealed our deal over a cigarette.

"Isn't this dangerous?" I asked."No," he reassured me in careful English. "Everybody does it when they're not taking bribes." He was a poet, he said, and this is how he supplements his income. He bought up foreign currency and turned the loot over to a clearing point, which then sold it to Czechs, who in turn used the money at import stores that accept only foreign currency.

If the Czech government only utilized half of the entrepreneurial spirit currently flourishing in the black market, its GNP would probably not be slowly sinking into the minus area."I have a question," said our waiter the next morning as we chewed bacon that could not possibly have ever been attached to a live animal. "You want caviar?" For breakfast? we thought, not fully awake. "Twenty dollars," he continued, pulling out of his pocket a large tin. We turned him down regretfully, thinking we'd better spend our mass of crowns to pay our hotel, whose outlandish rate per day had been cut to about $25 thanks to my street banking.

That's what we thought. What happened as we approached the hotel desk—well, Kafka would have rolled on the burgundy carpet.

The black-suited man seemed oddly confounded by the tatty heap of crowns in front of him. Visas, please, he said. Oh, sure, here. He looked at the visas carefully and then shook his head. Only then did we realize that all official exchanges were entered on our visas. And according to our visas, we only had the small amount of crowns we'd been required to change at the border. Any other crowns did not, could not, exist, even though they lay there in stacks on the counter. He would not accept them.

Beet-red in the face, very annoyed, we handed over a credit card to pay the balance. So what to do with the excess crowns? There wasn't a human being in Czechoslovakia who would want to buy back crowns. It was forbidden to bring Czech money out of the country.

The solution came to us in a flash. Why not *give* it away, we thought. Why not give away the $100 worth of crowns (an average two weeks wage) to the most perfect and deserving babushka we met on the trek back to the border? And on a side road we found her: dressed completely in black from the scarf on her head to the big boats lashed to her ankles. She was at least 90 years old and was carrying home a pitcher of beer.

We stopped and politely asked the way to Vienna. She smiled and pointed, presumably not understanding a word. So we thanked her for the information and put into her gnarled, veined hand the pile of money. Her one tooth nearly popped out of her face. She stared at the big foreign car. She stared at us. She stared at the money. She looked at the sky. Then she smiled again and thrust the pitcher through the window. "Drink," she said, "drink."

So we sat and drank our $100 beer. It was a great beer, the woman was happy, the memory remains grotesquely vivid. In some weird way, it was a fair rate of exchange.

Observations and questions

1) Writers and reporters routinely confront complex ethical decisions.

   A) Hoelterhoff must decide how to present her illegal activities to her readers. Do you think she acted responsibly given the conditions under which she was working?

   B) She is asked not to write anything about dissident artists in Prague. Discuss the various dimensions of this ethical problem. Do you think the writer made the right decisions?

2) The lead contains several interesting elements worthy of discussion:

   A) The writer plunges *in medias res,* into the middle of things. "We still had a kilometer or so to go...." The word *kilometer* places the reader in a foreign setting, and the first clause gets the reader moving with the writer.

   B) The first sentence is *cumulative.* Subject and verb come at the beginning. The sentence then accumulates elements. Even a long sentence with such a structure reads clearly.

   C) Concrete elements serve as symbols for life in Czechoslovakia: *barbed wire, watchtowers and closely trimmed meadows.*

   D) Contrasting images help the writer establish a focus for the story: *squadron* plays off *field mice; baby-faced* plays off *machine guns.*

3) Writers should not leave holes in stories, important unexplained bits of information. Do you

know what Charter 77 is? Does the writer ever tell you? Can you discern it from context?

4) Discuss the episode of the old woman that concludes the story. The writer could have gone on in this chronology, telling the reader how she got out of Czechoslovakia. Which ending would you prefer?

5) Novelist Milan Kundera describes life in Prague as a "black comedy." Hoelterhoff uses dark comedy throughout as a means of commenting on life in this city. For example, the guard who takes her magazine away becomes "the Warsaw Pact's expert on herpes...." Discuss other such examples in the story.

6) Hoelterhoff likes to use the endings of paragraphs to make emphatic points and to reward the reader. The phrases "machine guns," "a beefy, Stalinist face," and "tales of horror in dimly lit rooms" all come at the ends of paragraphs. Read your own work to see if you use this technique effectively.

Manuela Hoelterhoff at work*

In August 1982 I found myself in Europe to review the "documenta" in Germany, which happens once every four years. To make the trip cost effective, I tried to find other articles to work on. Since I speak German, I looked for places where I could travel and raise as little suspicion as possible to get a story.

I decided to go to Vienna to write about refugee camps there. I found myself with extra time and thought it would be interesting to compare Vienna and Prague. Before World War I, these two cities had a contest of "which one is the prettiest." The question at the time was not easily answered. Many considered Prague architecturally the more satisfying and beautiful.

Given the divergent political and economic histories of these two cities since World War I, I had before me a rare possibility. I could contrast two political systems and how they have affected life, art and architecture in two cities that were once so interrelated.

So after spending several days in Vienna, I went to Prague on a Thursday evening. I went through that gruesome border, where they confiscated my magazine with the "Herpes" cover story. This was read assiduously by the border guards, which was very amusing.

In Czechoslovakia I was going to focus on the artistic life of the city. I had several phone numbers of artists with me. They had been given to me by an American collector of Czech art. It turned out that the collector had misunderstood whom I was writing for. The artists, who were expecting me, were later extremely distressed to learn that I was with the *Wall Street Journal*, the organ of capitalism.

Transcribed and edited from a recorded interview.

I subsequently received an urgent letter, smuggled out via Italy, begging me not to write up any interviews or mention any names. Publicity would cause severe repercussions for these artists, who work outside the official academic structure, but are tolerated because they bring in currency.

As a result, I was faced with either hurting people who had been friendly to me or restructuring my article. Fortunately, the journey had been fraught with such grotesque humor, that restructuring proved not very difficult to do. The dilemma enriched the article in ways I had not foreseen. I decided not to write about the artists, except in passing.

I had no problem in taking notes and photographs in Prague. I was aware that the hotel was being watched and that it was not advisable to use the telephone. I did exercise some care. I took only tiny little pads with me that I could stick in the pocket of my jeans. The point is, you really don't know what to expect.

The lead, "We still had a kilometer or so to go...," was my way of creating atmosphere and putting myself in the story at the start. I prefer to write from an "I" viewpoint. "I" would emphasize that this was a personal journey.

I cannot write anything without a lead. That's what takes an extraordinary amount of time. Sometimes I think I waste it, but then I think it's part of this peculiar writing process I've developed. I'm incapable of doing anything unless I have a solid first paragraph and even the last few lines of the story.

With my lead I could do a chronological reporting of the trip from the moment I passed into Prague. I could tell practically every fascinating detail that happened to me.

I didn't want to repeat the border crossing at the end. The old woman provided a richer, more satisfying, conclusion. She was the last citizen of Czechoslovakia I encountered.

The experience had been so peculiar, and in its own grotesque way, so wonderful. As I was writing, I knew all along that the old crone dressed in black was the ending. The article came to a natural conclusion.

I'm usually pretty good about beginnings and endings. The problem is always the middle. What do you leave in and what do you take out? Where is your emphasis?

I'm really a bad deadline writer. I don't write quickly at all. I take enormous amounts of notes. Then I need three days, at least, of absolute quiet to go through the notes.

The first step is to make a list of the points I have to cover. The next step is to make an outline, to put the points in some kind of order.

I do all this in longhand. There's a real manual approach. I sit down with real pieces of paper, a pen or a pencil, and plot it.

Then I sit and type, which is a big chore for me because I can't type either. I've never learned some of the basic crafts of journalism. See, it's possible to become a writer even if you can't type.

A conversation with
Manuela Hoelterhoff

CLARK: When did you come to the United States?

HOELTERHOFF: In the mid '50s. I was born in 1949. My father came in '55 or '56 because he thought the streets were paved with gold. He later discovered that this was not quite the case.

Did you grow up speaking German?

Yes. I'm bilingual, which is why I'm so afraid of interviews, I think. I worry that I'll get the syntax wrong. I made an attempt to learn English on the big boat coming over. Then I had to learn it. I entered the second grade, I must have been barely 8. Kids can be very cruel. You have to learn quickly. So I learned to speak pretty much without an accent.

There's an interesting tradition in English literature of great writers—like Nabokov and Conrad—for whom English was not a first language. I've also taught foreign language students who wound up having greater control and respect for the language than native speakers.

I think that's possible. I remember even late in high school, when I realized I had to get certain grades to go to college, that I would sit down with books of synonyms and try to expand my vocabulary. I think not knowing what certain words are, you enrich your vocabulary by learning a variety of words. I would have to go to the dictionary. Often I would pick up two words for what I was looking for and they would stick in my head. You come to reflect more on the meaning of words because they are still new to you so you try to figure out what they really mean.

When did you start writing in a serious way?

By writing for the college paper, the *Hofstra Chronicle,* I assembled a large portfolio of writing before I was 21. I got a lot of bad writing out of the way early. They let me do whatever I wanted because they thought I was extremely weird, and they were not going to tussle with someone who brought in opera reviews.

The first magazine article I published was in William F. Buckley's *National Review.* He has that wonderful command of English, a very polished style, a very large vocabulary. There I went quite wild for a couple of articles. And that was the first encouragement I got. Buckley was very sweet. Every time I would publish something he would send a very nice curt little note: "Well done." It was a response I appreciated.

That portfolio of Hofstra work also got me into the Institute of Fine Arts. They looked at the writing and saw that occasionally there was a thought glimmering behind the words.

You write about architecture, art, opera and television. Did your specialized knowledge come from studies at the Institute? From personal reading?

Both. Opera I've loved since I was about 13 or 14. It's the one area of music I am well acquainted with. I know what's going on in the opera world. But I will not write about any other aspect of music. That would be pretentious. At the Institute, I studied art and architecture.

You don't seem to be afraid to handle a topic that may allow you to stretch your wings.

I'll tell you why that can be. It has to do with where I work. There's no one here looking over my shoulder, putting the proverbial gun to my head saying, "You must write one piece this week." If you have the leisure that we have here, I think it encourages a bit of roaming. It's sort of a Renaissance approach.

I'm interested in your perception of your audience. Are you writing for people who voted for Reagan? (Just kidding.) A general audience? An audience of people who may know enough about art to recognize allusions to artists?

For many years, I did not think about my audience at all. I used to assume that the only one who read what I wrote would be my mother. It's really strange. I had no perception of the *Journal's* readership at all, which is probably good because it kept me free. By now I won't say that I don't care, but a certain style has been established.

I think I always assumed I was writing for a fairly educated audience, but one that was not specialized in any field. We are also writing to a national audience that does not see many of the shows that I write about. So I have adopted— actually it came naturally—a kind of descriptive approach. I hope there's some undercurrent of criticism there, or a critical viewpoint, but it is an anecdotal, coloristic approach to writing that describes the event. What it was. What it could have been. How it compared to previous events.

In a way, the two pieces here combine travel and criticism. Are you developing a new genre? There are elements of narrative, description and elements of exposition as well.

I'm always interested in how art gets produced or whom art was produced for. I'm interested in

the socio-economic background. So I will never
write in a formalist way. By that I mean I will
never go to an art show and describe the paintings as they exist themselves. I want to know who
the person is. I want to know about biography.
If I were talking about abstract expressionism, I
want to know about the '40s and '50s. That kind
of brings you out of the gallery. We like history
here, so I read a lot of history. For instance, I'm
reviewing a Holbein show. Holbein painted the
court of Henry VIII. So I've got a biography here
of Henry VIII. I have a new biography of Sir
Thomas More. I'm going to write as much about
the people as about Holbein the artist.

**I see a lot of impressive reporting in these
pieces. Do you think being a good reporter
makes you a better critic? Do you take a lot
of notes?**

Yes. And I photograph a lot, too. I document
everything I see. I take enormous amounts of
notes. Even for these reviews, I do a lot of interviews with an artist or with a director of a show.
A lot of leg work does go into it. Often I find it
excruciating, because by nature I am not shy, but
retiring. I really have to force myself to do it. It
would be much easier to just pop into the
"documenta," see the show, and write about the
art. It would be a typical art review. Who wants
that?

**When I used to review films, my motto was:
"The worse the movie, the better the review."
It was always harder to write interesting and
clever pieces on good films.**

It's so much easier to write cutting pieces. And
they are the ones that get remembered. It's unfortunately true that people will remember
unkind descriptions—John Simon writing about
Judy Garland's face—more than descriptions of
great beauty and success.

You seem to be able to exercise the same degree of ingenuity and style on praise as you can on negative criticism.

I hope often with a bit of wryness. I did a piece on still life painting last Thursday. I loved the show. All it was was paintings of zucchini and pomegranates and peaches. I was amused by the show and entertained by it, so I got an amusing and interesting piece out of it.

Isn't there a general perception of critics— that you can't please them, that they are always sarcastic and acerbic?

I try to go to the opera a lot. I see every new production, often cast changes. I see 10 times more than the average opera goer. I'm going to be more easily bored and annoyed. There's no getting around that. You cannot bring that almost naive enthusiasm to an encounter that is average. But it might work perfectly nicely for a couple that may go to the opera maybe four or five times a year. Now the idea is not to spoil it for them, but your obligation is also to make clear that this is an average evening, and let's not forget it.

What do you see as your primary role. Is it as someone who tries to elevate standards?

Oh, God. Elevate standards. No. (Laughs.) I've given up on that a long time ago. To jostle people into awareness. If we do that, that's more than sufficient. If we keep them away from something absolutely awful, I think we're doing our job. If we encourage people to go to something that's worthwhile, we've done our job. And beyond that, I have no expectations.

I'm intrigued by the way some writers are able to create images, metaphors, analogies which seem apt. I have a feeling that part of it is just hard work, thinking and thinking

and writing and casting aside a lot of images that don't work until you find the right one. Where do yours come from?

They leap out of the word processor at some point. A few writers have an amazing gift for metaphor. There's a natural facility that natural writers have, people born with a pen in their hand.

I was not. I think initially I used writing as a way of expressing myself on paper in a way I was unable to do in conversation. For me writing was a release, something almost physically satisfying.

It started at Hofstra where I would scribble, scribble, scribble. I still do that. I really struggle for those metaphors, and I struggle for interesting allusions.

Do you have some feeling when you're writing that, "Here is where I need one"? Do you say here's where I need an image that describes exactly that this art catalogue was like— "...a street map to Kabul"?

I look for ways of saying something that are not ordinary. I could have said the catalogue is too large and confusing. But would you remember that? I don't think so.

Rushworth Kidder

Finalist, Commentary

RUSHWORTH KIDDER is a columnist for the *Christian Science Monitor*. Since 1979 he has written columns, news stories and personal essays for the *Monitor*. He served as that paper's London correspondent and has been traveling and writing about Central America. Kidder came to journalism from Wichita State University where he was associate professor of English for 10 years. He graduated from Amherst College in 1965 and has a Ph.D. from Columbia University. He has written books on Dylan Thomas and E.E. Cummings.

Window seat

DECEMBER 6, 1982

In the old days it would have been called a "crack" train—the once-a-day special pounding south from Toronto to New York City. The railway company, with a certain poetic flourish, has given it a name: Maple Leaf. These days, however, 11 hours and 32 minutes somehow seems less "crack" than it used to; and when I boarded the Maple Leaf at Albany the other evening, it was clear that there weren't many of us who still shared that delicate mix of nostalgia, civility, and leisure necessary for train travel in an airport age.

So I had, from the outset, half a car to myself. Now, that's a disorienting circumstance: I've been wedged into so many coach-class airline seats in this country, and settled for so many aisle seats on British Rail trains, that I've come to think of traveling as a gregarious and demotic sport. Suitcase in hand, I wandered down the empty, darkened coach (they were changing engines, and we boarded in the semi-gloom of emergency lights), tried several locations that were not to my taste, and finally came upon an alcove whose two pairs of seats faced each other. I chose the forward-facing window seat, hoping the lights inside might be subdued enough to let me glimpse the Hudson River.

But the train pulled out, and the lights came up full, and the window was nothing but a gloss of reflections. I had books and papers at my side, yet nothing called out to be read. So I sat and thought. That, after all, is what trains are good for: promising ample time, they are havens for procrastinators, dreamers, and those who have found the link between idleness and insight.

I found myself recalling a similar alcove a few years ago on a train from London to Scotland. I was with my wife (who likes sitting forward rather than backward) and we were rolling through Yorkshire pastureland in broad daylight. I had recently come (through the bizarre logic that sometimes characterizes changes in career) out of an academic life teaching poetry and into journalism; and I recall thinking that, given my new-found occupation, I was in the wrong seat. Looking backward, I saw only what had just gone by. It occurred to me that I should be sitting where my wife was, that journalism, wedded to the workaday world and intent on spotting trends before they crest, should take the seat on the train facing forward. The backward-looking seat—leisured, contemplative, and rooted in an academic turn of mind that ponders the ever-deepening past—belongs to history. To be sure, both journalists and historians do a good deal of rubbernecking over their shoulders. But their natural pose is straight ahead—the journalist keen to identify the speck on the horizon before it hurtles into the present, the historian content to wait until the massive object that once filled the window recedes and takes its place among the other objects of the landscape.

The metaphor came and went, I recall, and I had only time for a tremor of suspicion at its overly neat two-part structure before something—a herd of sheep, perhaps—sparked a comment from my wife and I craned round to see. So it was not until the other night along the Hudson that I came back to the analogy. What was it, I thought, that had made me slightly uneasy?

I was pondering that point when, for reasons I never did learn, the lights on the Maple Leaf suddenly blacked out. The train rolled on undisturbed, and soon a maintenance man clanked up the aisle and disappeared into the rear of the diesel engine. I looked out the window. There, dimly lit under the cloudy night, was the river, and beyond it the lights of a town on the far shore and the low mountains so beloved of the painters of the Hudson River School.

It was a glorious sight—mysterious, evocative, yet altogether gentle. I spent some moments looking straight out the window, nose close to the glass. Then, with a jolt made all the ruder by its absolute silence, the lights came on again. River, town, mountains, and sky vanished. I was staring, instead, at a reflection of myself.

Startled, I drew back—but not before, in an instant's illumination, I saw what had troubled me in the earlier analogy. What it lacked, I saw, was a third element: the sense of the now. If journalism looks forward and history backward, who is watching that illusive evanescence we call the present?

With the question came the answer: the poet.

I sat back with the same relief Dr. Watson must have felt when Sherlock Holmes explained a missing link in an unsolved case. The poet, indeed—the one who catches in sharp detail that moment when the future is just sliding into the past—must always sit sideways, face to the glass. He can glance forward (more readily than the historian) or backward (with greater ease than the journalist)—but only at the risk of losing forever the fleeting image of the now.

I pondered the idea, slowly, carefully. And as I did, I began to see why I had been content to leave the haven of the academy for the hurly-burly of journalism. For modern poetry, I realized, tends to miss the mark. Poetry has always, perhaps, ridden the Midnight Special of the mind. But for centuries the lights inside were dim; and if the poet's own face showed up in the glass, the reflection was not bright enough to obscure the vision of the world beyond. But these days, it seems, the lights inside are at full glare; the poet, searching vainly for an outer world, sees only himself. Solipsistic, self-enwrapped, he comes to see poetry less as a charting of the world's play upon the soul than as a mirror for the ego.

Dear reader, if I have chosen journalism, do not take me for a Philistine. I love poetry—I would not write you this way if I did not. Nor, by "poetry," do I mean some hideously impersonal versifying of a merely objective world. I know full well that the self really does matter— that true poetry is born at those illusive borders where the river of individual consciousness laps against the world's shore, where future dissolves into past.

No, I am only calling for balance, for an art that sees beyond the self. I long for a poetry that looks through the same window and into the same world that the journalist and the historian see and know. We are all of us, after all, on the same train.

Observations and questions

1) Ezra Pound once defined poetry as "news that stays news." Consider Kidder's essay in the context of that definition.

2) Read Michael Berryhill's essay "The Lede & the Swan" in the March 1983 issue of *The Quill.* Berryhill argues that good poets and good reporters have much in common. Kidder himself reads, writes and thinks about poetry. In what sense can his writing be called poetic? In what sense journalistic? Are the two ever in conflict?

3) Many films and novels use trains symbolically. Discuss the symbolism of trains and consider how Kidder is consistent or in conflict with the literary and cinematic traditions.

4) In the first paragraph, Kidder writes "The railway company, with a certain poetic flourish, has given it a name: the Maple Leaf." Having read the essay, do you think the writer was planting a clue in that first graph that the piece would be about poetry? Is this too subtle to work on the reader?

5) A common technique for both writers and film makers is the flashback. In this essay the writer moves from the present back to a train ride in Scotland. Discuss how the writer moves in and out of this scene.

6) Exactly half way through the essay comes the sentence, "What was it, I thought, that had made me slightly uneasy?" Notice how this serves as a hook for the reader, a midpoint boost that moves the reader into the second half of the story. The reader has some incentive to continue, to discover what made the writer uneasy.

7) Notice the passage, "Dear reader, if I have chosen journalism, do not take me for a Philistine." Does this sentence seem corny and impossibly old-fashioned to you? Is it delivered tongue-in-cheek? Is it in keeping with the style and content of the essay?

On keeping an open mind

APRIL 7, 1982

We have few differences, my wife and I. To be sure, she pronounces the *i* in *neither* and leans toward orange instead of grapefruit juice. But we agree on most things except a certain matter of domestic architecture. For she loves modern houses and I love doors. And between the two, it seems, there is a great gulf fixed.

Contemporary architects, I have noticed, don't much care for doors. They only seem to use them where nothing else will do—at entrances, for example, or on bathrooms. So the modern house, like the American plains in the days of the bison, is a thing of great undivided spaces. The open reaches sweep from kitchen into dining area, roll on unbroken into the living room, and cascade over a step or two into the family room. Between kitchen and dining area, for example, lies a distinction as blurred as that between late winter and early spring. Standing in the midst of either, one knows it to be different from the other; but one is never just sure where the boundary is.

So at the risk of sounding positively Cenozoic in my fondness for times past, let me argue the case for doors. First, I suppose, I must explain that I grew up in a house full of them. Our kitchen alone had nine—all solidly built paneled affairs with sturdy porcelain knobs. My respect for them dates from the day our cleaning lady washed the kitchen floor at snack time and then departed. Undaunted, I mounted the hall door, feet on the knobs and hands grasping the top, and swung myself into the kitchen to the counter. Then I stepped across the stove, swung across on the broom closet door to the pantry, and availed myself of several fig newtons—with not a single toe print on her still-wet floor. The old doors, fastened like Excalibur into the rock of their spruce frames, never so much as sighed.

It was in that same kitchen that we perform-ed a ritual twice a year. Every fall, as the north wind whistled around the back porch, we put up the black wooden storm door. And each spring the screen door reappeared. It generally had some repairs pending: for our dog, a hybrid hound whose exuberance exceeded his patience, fancied it a mere mirage. On summer days, seized by the sound of a foreign cat outside, he would boil out from under the table and rip through the doorway—whereupon the screen door would fly back in amazement with a great twanging of its spring, to slam shut again well behind his tail. Nor was his return trip any challenge. The wooden crosspieces were on the outside of the door; he would grab the one below the handle in his teeth, pull open the door until he could stick in a paw, and then flip back the door enough to wriggle through. He may have been silly but he wasn't stupid.

His partner at the water dish was a cat many years his senior, glossy and black with gold markings, like an old piano. By a kind of regal self-assurance and some very sharp claws, she had early squelched his penchant for insurrec-tion. She was, in fact, master of the house, so much so that she called forth what may have been my finest childhood invention.

The problem she and I faced was her restlessness. I kept my bedroom door shut against the hall light and she loved to sleep at the foot of my bed. But just as I was sliding toward sleep, she would decide to go elsewhere. Moreover, she was the one with patience: she would set the timer of her meower every seven seconds and let it go off with devilish regularity until I lumbered to the door. One night amid such tumbling the invention hit me: an electric door opener. Finding a solenoid from a discarded washing machine, I fastened it to a kind of lever on the inside doorknob, and wired it back to a doorbell button beside my bed. The solenoid would yank down the lever and release the latch, whereupon a rubber band, fastened between door and baseboard, would swing the door slowly open. It worked fine, with only a couple of problems. One was the noise: for the solenoid, made to jerk great greasy washing machine gears into place, was overqualified for the job. More than once it terrified family members who, tapping like Poe's raven at my chamber door, were greeted with a great blast of buzzing magnets and crashing metal, followed by silence and the slow, mysterious opening of the door. The other problem, of course, was that the operation was irreversible. Having triumphantly let the cat out, I always had to get up to shut the door again.

I guess, in some ways, I've been shutting doors ever since. For I have great respect for them. In old New England houses they had a purpose: they kept the heat, always a scarce commodity, just where it was wanted. Only with the advent of central heating did people begin taking them down and storing them in barns—to be rediscovered by the children of a more fuel-conscious age.

But if doors had a purpose, they also had a fringe benefit. They produced privacy, quietness, the solitude that breeds deep thought. I realize that it cannot quite be proved that the tradition of academic excellence in New England is directly a function of the region's number of doors. In fact, however, few scholars could survive a doorless existence. The ability to close off the intrusive and the distracting—to shut out all the bustle of the senses—is the first prerequisite to deep thought.

Or so I used to think. Recently, however, I have felt a change coming on. Maybe it stems from my job: my desk now sits in the middle of a newsroom, surrounded by phones and conversations. The people I most admire know how to write in the midst of 50 different noises, all of them intriguing. They have taught me a great lesson: that there are ways, if the physical door is lacking, to shut the mental door.

I'm not a master of that discipline. I still find within myself too much of the dog, bolting after every cat that passes on the far side of the screen door of my mind. But I have at least seen the promise—that concentration is a habit of thought and not an accident of place, and that a warm and open sociableness brings as much benefit as a cloistered solitude.

I'm not about to shift my pronunciation of *neither*. But I'm getting more interested in modern houses.

Observations and questions

1) Good titles can help the reader (and the writer) understand the central meaning of a story. The title "On Keeping an Open Mind" was written by an editor. Do you think it reflects the focus of the story? Can you think of a different title that might be more effective?

2) Rarely do formal essays appear in newspapers. We see essays, of a sort, produced by columnists and editorial writers. But few are quite so formal as this. Study the history of the essay as a genre. Read examples from Montaigne to E. B. White. Now discuss the place of the essay in daily journalism. Are there some topics for which the form seems best suited? How can the essay relate to the world of news and events?

3) The word *essay* derives from a French word meaning "a trial, an attempt." The writer says, in essence, I am trying here to discover meaning. Consider Kidder's work in light of that etymology.

4) Students of writing often talk about *voice* in an essay. *Voice* refers to the illusion that the writer is speaking directly to the reader, that you can "hear" the writer in the words. How would you describe the *voice* in this essay? Look at your own writing and consider the *voice* there.

5) *Voice* relates to *audience*. Examine the language and style of this piece and speculate for what audience it was intended. Can a responsible journalist write only for an affluent, erudite audience, or should he always strive to reach the greatest number of readers?

6) Kidder's paragraphs are long, at least by newspaper standards. Are they too long? Do they present the reader with impenetrable blocks of gray type? Are there logical places within longer paragraphs where they could be broken up?

7) Trace the transitions and logical connections that tie together the disparate ideas and anecdotes in the essay. How does the writer get from his wife to doors to animals to open-mindedness?

8) A door is a basic human archetype. A rock group is called The Doors. Opportunity knocks but once. And Jesus said "Knock and it shall be opened unto you." Explore the word *door* in the *Oxford English Dictionary* and in collections of famous quotations. See if you can find some connotations that would have enhanced Kidder's story.

9) Kidder uses the word *Cenezoic* in this piece, and uses the words *gregarious*, *demotic* and *solipsistic* in the other. Are these words understandable from context or are they likely to be above the majority of readers?

10) Consider the effect on the reader of the following images:
    ...the modern house, like the American plains in the days of the bison...
    ...The old doors, fastened like Excalibur into the rock of their spruce frames...
    ...a cat...glossy and black with gold markings, like an old piano.
    ...she would set the timer of her meower every seven seconds and let it go off.
    ...tapping like Poe's raven at my chamber door.

Rushworth Kidder at work

I have an older friend who paints watercolor landscapes—vigorous, bright scenes finished before the paper is half dry. He sells them for vigorous, bright prices, too, which now and then bring arch looks and skeptical comments. "Howlongdit takya ta paint that?" he is often asked. To which he replies, with serene self-confidence, "About 40 years."

I guess that's true for writing as well. I have a fairly good idea why I wrote "On Keeping an Open Mind"; but I can't for the life of me say how long it took to compose it. All my life, I suppose—although, in the end, I spent about three hours writing.

It grew out of a conversation with my wife about the doorlessness of present-day houses. Her instincts are much more contemporary than mine: she has a natural affinity for modern art, where I still have to labor to like the truly avant-garde. At the time, we lived in a 240-year-old house chock-full of doors, which I rather fancied and she thought a bit stale. But it was a great conversation piece; and the more we talked about its merits and drawbacks, the more I found myself arguing for its doorishness.

As I explain in the essay, I had grown up among doors. What I don't explain is that I had also grown up in an academic family where to study meant to be quiet —and to be quiet meant to shut the door. I think I probably carried that to something of an extreme in college—squirreling myself away in library attics, even setting up a secret desk in the basement of a deserted campus building whose upper floors were being systematically demolished by the wrecker's ball. As I headed toward my chosen career as a university professor, that's how I defined myself: a needer of quietness.

Yet here I was, after a decade of teaching writing and poetry, plunged into a life of journalism. Like everyone else in this business, I've written my share of stories in airports, at deli counters, and in phone booths. And I've had to read—and understand, fast—wire-service dispatches in the middle of a newsroom babbling with noisy energy. It hasn't been easy; but it has been a transition.

At the time of our discussion about doors, I guess I hadn't caught on to the extent of the transition. But the more I thought about it later, the less sense my defense of doors made—or, to put it another way, the less I could afford to let it make sense. My wife was too kind to mention it; but she might have won her point simply by saying, "Accept your major premise, and you destroy your new-found career. You may never again have an office with a door on it."

So there it was: a paradox of small but highly personal proportions, a contradiction which (once I had recognized it) demanded resolution. Exactly the sort of challenge that lends itself to an essay—if it could be brought down to earth. What it needed, clearly, was a range of solid detail upon which to anchor its more metaphysical meaning—without which it would sink into an abyss of laborious philosophizing which makes such frightfully difficult reading.

In this case, obviously, the source of detail would be the doors themselves—solid, describable things, and commonplace enough. The strategy, too, was fairly evident: lest the readers doze over heavy abstractions in the opening paragraphs (and drift away into other, more lively prose), best sneak up on the main point. It's a technique I use frequently in essays, though rarely in straight journalism: Come in sideways (the opening sentences about the differences between my wife and me), straighten out into the ostensible topic (doors), and then, having gathered speed across that runway of detail, lift off into a discussion of its significance.

I can never plan the lift-off, either. The detail, yes: I block that out ahead of time, arranging the flow of incidents before I even approach the typewriter. They take on their own life, however, as I write. And it is out of that life that the ending springs. The dog, for example: he got into this essay simply by virtue of the screen door. It wasn't until he was actually on the page that I saw how well he led into the cat—and that he was the link that got me from kitchen to bedroom. Nor did I have so much as a hint of the undisciplined-dog metaphor at the end until, all at once, I was writing it out. That's what I mean by lift-off: That's what makes writing a process of discovery.

And those are the kinds of discoveries that make writing sing. Not that the writing should bubble up effortlessly out of some magical sub-conscious, and that all you need do is sit back and wait to be inspired. Far from it. The writers I most admire are highly skillful people, with a keen sense of discipline and consistency and a sharply self-critical eye. But mostly they are people who love words, who place no limits on the power of words, who recognize that there are whole stylistic galaxies out there which their skills, however powerful, have not even touched. They are people who love to write—and, even more, love to revise.

Yet they're also people who recognize that the writer, looking at one thing, sees another. That's what makes metaphor. And the making of metaphor —the revealing of the interconnections between otherwise unrelated images—is itself the process of discovery. If I thought that the central part of my writing were simply the recording of ideas I had been responsible for dreaming up, I would be terrified of failure—or bored beyond words. But I've watched too many essays happen to think that. One doesn't sit down to write out what's already been thought up. One writes to open up thought.

A conversation with
Rushworth Kidder

CLARK: Where did these two columns come from?

KIDDER: The *Monitor's* Home Forum page is a page of essays, poetry and painting. It's at the back end of the paper every day. It also has the *Monitor's* single religious article each day. Through this page, we publish more poetry per year than any other periodical in the country because we do it day after day.

So people come to the page with the regular expectation of having some opportunities to enjoy literature?

It's the more reflective, perhaps the more subjective part of the newspaper. It's where you talk about what you are thinking inside, rather than what is going on in the world outside. It is a freelance page, even for people who work on the paper.

It seems like it would be a wonderful place for young staff writers to try something different or off-beat.

To some extent, especially the younger writers who are trying out their style and are not quite sure where they're going. But most of the writers are from elsewhere. We get contributions from all around the world.

We just ran a series on poets. I've written several of them. I did one on Wallace Stevens and one on Dylan Thomas and one on Yeats. It's a matter of finding someone who can talk about those poets without being pedantic. Someone who won't make it into a piece of academic literary criticism, but who can say, "Here's why Yeats feels the way he feels" to someone who is sensitive about feelings.

What are the differences in style when you are addressing a general rather than a strictly academic audience?

I've thought about that a lot because my background is in academics. I spent 10 years as a university professor. My field was 20th century literature. Writing academic criticism is necessary and terribly useful. I don't mean to scorn that, but it has a limited audience. It is written for other people interested professionally in the work you are studying. There's a great body of people beyond that who have a genuine fascination with words and a real interest in poetry. Mostly you want to capture their attention, to show them that these are not poets writing only for other poets. These are people trying to articulate a sense of the world that matters to all of us.

What is your sense of the audience for your essays?

I guess the sense is of a literate, lay audience. Not specialized, not professional readers, but nevertheless people who tend to be very interested in words and the way language works, who really enjoy a good read.

My friend Peter Meinke is a poet who has taught in Poland. He says that in Poland the newspapers are nothing, but that you could fill a stadium to hear certain poets. And in the USA the newspapers are important, but who reads poetry? He blames it, in part, on the poets. He believes American poetry is inaccessible to most readers.

In a sense that's what I was trying to get at in "Window Seat." I don't have too much patience

with Gertrude Stein and I guess I even struggle
with people like Ezra Pound. I, too, have a great
love for the sorts of poetry that make clear sense.
And as a journalist now, I see more and more the
fact that there are vast numbers of people out
there for whom poetry has become wholly irrele-
vant. That saddens me because somehow one
needs to get back to the sense that words do matter and have the harmony and the musicality of
a real art.

**I want to read to you from an article that ap-
peared in a recent issue of *The Quill*
magazine. Michael Berryhill writes, "Unlike
Walt Whitman, who dropped journalism and
became a poet, I am a poet who has turned
to the teaching and occasional practice of
journalism. I haven't had to abandon poetry
because nothing in its writing is incompati-
ble with journalism. Good writing in poetry
has more in common with good writing in
journalism than it does with bad writing in
poetry." How would you react to that?**

I think he's right on there. I think what he's dealing with is the quality of the language, and the
way that words work. My difficulty is that I
always want to write sooner than I should. I'm
interested in the process of writing. If there's one
thing I must keep reminding myself, it's to make
sure that I've done all the research. The further
I get into the story, the more I see how it can be
shaped, the whole thing begins to come together
in my head, and I find myself getting impatient
to get at it, to get to the part I think is most thrill-
ing. A lot of journalists are interested in the thrill
of the chase, learning the gossip, and from talking with them I discover that many don't really
look forward to the writing.

**Where do the ideas for these essays come
from? Do you begin with a concrete thing and
move to the level of ideas? Or do you**

begin with an abstract notion and look for concrete details to illustrate it?

As to where it begins, I don't know. It seems to me to begin an awful long time ago. A lot of my essays go back to childhood and pick up examples from the past. Quite often they will start with a paradox, some kind of contradiction that strikes me as odd, that I would like to resolve.

Is that what happened in "Window Seat"?

Obviously having gone from a tenured position in a university to a career in journalism—you don't make that kind of move without a fair amount of thought as to who one is and where one is going and why it matters.

So the question of poetry as opposed to journalism has not been far from my thought for a number of years. So you've got all that brewing around underneath and perhaps a need to come to terms with it.

It's because that stuff is underneath that one finds—when one is sitting on a train—the beginnings of this essay. You sit in a little alcove and suddenly it dawns on you that there is a metaphor here for your own human experience.

Thinking through that metaphor at that time brought me almost to the point of having something to say, but not quite. Not having thought of that metaphor for two years, the next step occurred when I got on that train in Albany.

I have discovered that one of the most fruitful times to do this kind of writing is when I am traveling. I've done an awful lot of writing on planes. I so enjoy the process of writing, nothing makes time pass more rapidly than to be actually engaged in composition.

There was something of that when I got on the train in Albany. I remember thinking, "Oh, good. Here's a couple of hours. I'm not necessarily going to write but I really don't have anything else to do. I can think and construct an essay,

if one happens to come along, in my head.
Perhaps in a week or two I can write it out."

It's not a question, at this point, of writing
it word for word. It's a question of blocking,
perhaps the way a theater director would.

Can you describe what you mean by "blocking"?

I am talking about the significant chunks of
meaning. What interested me was that
metaphor, of sitting in the alcove, one facing forward, one facing backward—and finally the third
element (the poet staring sideways out the
window).

What made it worth explaining was the
realization that dawned on me, probably in the
course of three or four minutes. It was both an
intellectual recognition that here was the third
element of this metaphor, and a feeling that came
along and said, "Yes, that's it." I then had to go
further with it and ask myself, "So what?" So
one has this metaphor for the way the world
works. What is that telling us about the nature
of reality? How do we connect that to larger
issues? Typically, that kind of thinking comes as
I am in the process of writing. In that sense, the
process of writing is a tremendous act of self-
discovery.

When might you begin the actual writing of the first draft?

If I had to do it schematically, I generally begin
writing at the point which I have almost word
for word in my head the lead sentence and the
way out of that into the rest of the essay.

Then follows a sense of metaphor: What is
going to be the central kernel towards which I'm
moving in the piece. I may have some sense that
I can use several instances from my childhood.
That may account for the first half or two-thirds

of the piece. At the point I sit down to begin writing,
I really don't know where the thing is going to end.
And that is the process of self-discovery. And then,
of course, a lot of revising after that.

How much do you revise?

The writer who really likes to write is the writer
who likes to revise because it's at that point that
one finally gets the glory and the clarity of how
language works. You really get down to the nuts
and bolts of it. You ask yourself if you are going
to say *may* or *might*. It's at that point you go back
to the thesaurus or into the dictionary to discover
the second and third meanings of a word which the
reader may never catch but are there as a kind of
subtle reinforcement. I find the process of revision
tremendously rewarding. I write until the feel of
the rhythm of the sentence comes out the way it
ought to. It feels the way it ought to feel. Here is
the piece tapering down to its last final short
sentence .

**There is evidence that 75 percent of a writer's
time on a story is spent in planning and
rehearsal, activities which may come before
you sit in a chair and get your hands moving.**

Absolutely. It's one of the things, when I was
teaching, I tried to acquaint my students with, in
the simplest of terms. Here I am three weeks ahead
of time assigning a term paper. My point to them
always is, "For goodness sakes, don't wait until two
days before the paper is due to begin thinking
about it. Go home right now and think it through
to the point of saying, 'I know what it is I want
to write about.' And then you really can wait until the week before. But you will have the idea in
your head; it will dawn on you while you are
brushing your teeth, while you're walking around
campus, while you're getting your car out of the
parking lot. It will be part of you, and it will grow
on its own."

The unoriginal sin*

By ROY PETER CLARK

Each day in American newspapers and
magazines, journalists kidnap the words of other
writers without attribution or shame.

The practice is called plagiarism, a name
derived from the Latin word for kidnapper. In the
academic world, it is the most serious of crimes.
But in the world of journalism, a world without
footnotes, the snatching of words and ideas is too
often ignored, misunderstood or considered standard procedure.

Reporters plagiarize from novels, en-
cyclopedias, textbooks, magazines, wire stories,
syndicated columns, press releases, competing
newspapers and the morgue.

Some who commit the unoriginal sin are
charlatans. Others resort to it in moments of
pressure or personal crisis. Others slide into it
out of naivete or ignorance. They do not know
how much borrowing is too much, because
teachers and editors have failed to set limits and
suggest guidelines.

Enough examples of blatant plagiarism have
surfaced at good newspapers to make any con-
scientious editor wary.

• In 1975, a critic at the *Atlanta Constitution*
borrowed most of a film review from *Newsweek*.
Her editors chastised her. The woman claimed
to have a photographic memory. She begged to
be given another chance, and was. She did it
again and lost her job. "It was the stupidest kind
of plagiarism," remembers Ed Sears, now managing editor of the *Atlanta Journal and Constitu-*

---

*This article originally appeared in the March 1983 issue
of Washington Journalism Review. It is reprinted here by
permission of the editor.*

tion. "She took the stuff verbatim from a recent edition of *Newsweek.*"

• In 1978, a columnist for the *Charlotte News* kidnapped an old Art Buchwald column and published it under his own name. He was new to column writing, was responsible for five columns a week, and on a dry day resorted to wholesale plagiarism. An alert reader discovered it. The columnist apologized to his readers. He was moved to the copy desk.

• In 1980, a columnist for the Louisville *Courier-Journal* wrote a column on the economy described by one of his editors as "brilliant." This surprised no one as the writer had proven time and again that he was capable of such work. The paper was later notified by a lawyer that passages from the column were lifted from his client's book. The columnist admitted that he had read a review copy of the book, that he had been influenced by it, and that he had used it without attribution. Managing editor David Hawpe apologized for his columnist in print and eventually moved him to the copy desk.

• In 1981, a Los Angeles reporter for the Associated Press resigned after it was learned that her story about high speed races on California highways was both a composite and an act of plagiarism. Without attribution, the writer used several anecdotes and passages taken verbatim from *New West* magazine. She tricked the reader into thinking that she had witnessed the race described in *New West.*

• In February of 1982, the *New York Times* discovered that a free-lance writer had fabricated a story that appeared in the *New York Times Magazine.* Christopher Jones, 24, without leaving Spain, wrote an article that created the illusion he had visited remote regions of Cambodia and had caught a glimpse of Pol Pot. The hoax was uncovered when the *Village Voice* revealed that Jones' ending had been plagiarized from the Andre Malraux novel *The Royal Way.* Confronted by *Times* editors in Spain, Jones admitted that he had pilfered Malraux because "I needed a piece of color."

(As of this writing, the *New York Times Magazine* is investigating the accusation of "unacceptable borrowing" against another of its writers.)

• In 1972, shortly after becoming the editor of the *St. Petersburg Times,* Gene Patterson received a letter from the editor of *Better Homes and Gardens.* It contained a copy of an elaborate color drawing that had appeared in the *Times.* Attached to it was an identical piece of art from the magazine. "It made me heartsick," said Patterson. "It was a beautifully imaginative, very complicated color drawing. Our artist had copied it exactly, in every detail." He was fired. Plagiarism, obviously, is not confined to words. The way artists borrow from each other deserves its own investigation.

Almost every newspaper I have consulted offers an anecdote about serious plagiarism. I have heard of editorials copied word for word from the *New York Times* and government handouts. I have heard, but have not been able to verify, stories about a managing editor at a small paper who routinely plagiarized stories from newsmagazines, stole a whole series from a larger newspaper and even stuck his name over the work of his own reporters. Such a man might have inspired Samuel Johnson's famous piece of sarcasm: "Your manuscript is both good and original; but the part that is good is not original, and the part that is original is not good."

Plagiarism in newspapers (ethical plagiarism, that is, not the violation of copyright, which is a legal question) is more common than imagined and in many cases escapes detection. Most cases are cloudier and less spectacular than the ones cited above. Like defensive pass interference in football, they may be blatant or accidental, but they always deserve the yellow flag.

On September 1, 1982, Jerry Bledsoe, a columnist for the *Greensboro Daily News and*

Record, called me. He had just read *Best Newspaper Writing 1982*, an annual collection, which I edit, of the winning articles from the national writing competition sponsored by the American Society of Newspaper Editors (ASNE).

One of the stories, written by Tom Archdeacon of the *Miami News,* described Linda Vaughn, the buxom beauty queen of the racing car circuit. Bledsoe was attracted to the story because in 1975 he had written *The World's Number One, Flat-Out, All-Time Great Stock Car Racing Book,* which included a chapter on Linda Vaughn. When he read Archdeacon's story, Bledsoe was surprised to see some of his own words under Archdeacon's byline. He sent me a copy of his chapter, underlining 10 instances (about 100 words) in which Archdeacon had borrowed from him without attribution.

In 1975, Jerry Bledsoe had written: "To be a race queen is about the only way a woman can be involved in big time stock car racing." In 1981, Archdeacon changed only the tense: "To be a race queen was about the only way a woman could be involved in big time stock car racing."

The most damning passage was one in which Archdeacon used Bledsoe's language to describe the reaction of grimy mechanics to this voluptuous woman. In Bledsoe's words, the sight of her made them "stand in awe, made them punch one another in the ribs and giggle like little boys...." Archdeacon has them "stand in awe, bashful, punching each other in the ribs, giggling like school boys."

I wrote a report that was sent to ASNE seconding Bledsoe's cry of foul: "I believe that Tom Archdeacon is guilty of low-grade plagiarism and high-grade carelessness. There appears to be much original information in Archdeacon's story.... But the textual similarities speak for themselves. If Archdeacon were a student in my college English class, I'd give him a stern public lecture on the rules of plagiarism and make him write it again."

Bledsoe's phone call and my report set off a chain reaction. The ASNE contacted the *Miami News. Miami News* editors confronted Archdeacon. He later described the aftermath of that meeting in a report in the ASNE *Bulletin:* "It...had the effect of a baseball bat to the solar plexus. I spoke with them truthfully and quite frankly and then was excused from the room. I headed for my desk but never made it. I had to beeline for the bathroom, where I promptly threw up. And I haven't felt much better since."

Archdeacon told his editors that he admired Bledsoe's book, that he had used it for background on Linda Vaughn, and that under deadline he had confused Bledsoe's words with his own in more than 100 pages of sloppily taken notes. "I swear to God," Archdeacon wrote, "there was no deviousness intended."

Archdeacon flew to Greensboro to apologize to Bledsoe. They met for about 15 minutes in the newspaper coffee shop. "He was very contrite," says Bledsoe, "and I felt very sorry for him. It was a gray day and he was as downcast as the weather."

It was decided that Archdeacon would write a *mea culpa* for the November issue of the ASNE *Bulletin.* His publisher, David Kraslow, would declare that his writer had "made a serious error in judgment." And the ASNE board would chastise Archdeacon.

The board met in Washington, D.C., on October 21-22, and prepared a statement that read in part: "While what happened is a journalistic misdemeanor and not a felony—and appears to be a mistake rather than plagiarism—the board deplores that such gross carelessness and sloppiness could be part of the working procedure of such a talented writer." Archdeacon kept the award and his job.

In reviewing the case, it became clear to me that there is little agreement among journalists as to how the rules against plagiarism should af-

fect the behavior of reporters. Most newspapers
have no rules. Editors seem loath to define it,
especially in marginal cases. Plagiarism is the
skeleton in journalism's closet.

In preparing my report on Archdeacon, I
found nothing—no guidelines, no warnings, not
even the word *plagiarism* in indexes of the
newspaper stylebooks and journalism textbooks
on my shelf. I had to turn to English composition texts and handbooks for scholars for discussion on how much a writer can borrow.

Although most of the editors and senior staff
members of the *Miami News* thought Archdeacon
had blundered badly, the verdict was not
unanimous. In a memo to ASNE, publisher
Kraslow described the feeling of one dissenter,
"that Tom did what most journalists do routinely with research material—weave it into the body
of the story without attribution."

The ASNE board, according to three of its
members, did not easily come to a consensus on
whether Archdeacon had committed a mortal or
venial sin or what his penance should be. Nevertheless, "There was no thought of rescinding the
award," said Bob Stiff, editor of the St.
Petersburg *Evening Independent.* Still, these 20
top newspaper editors were hazy on the definition of plagiarism. "Well, how much borrowing
is too much?" Katherine Fanning, editor and
publisher of the *Anchorage Daily News,* asked
later. "Three words? Four words?"

The board accepted the notion that since the
borrowing was unintentional, the act was not
plagiarism. Jerry Bledsoe disagrees. "I think
they need to examine their standards," he said.
"I think that they've demeaned their awards."

Part of the problem is that all good reporters
compile, borrow and assimilate. "Writers do not
read for fun," writes T. S. Garp. They read for
work. They borrow juxtapositions, images,
metaphors, rhythms, puns, emphases, structures,
word orders, alliterations and startling facts.
They store these in their memory banks and in

their commonplace books. Months later these
words emerge in a new context and with personal
meaning, having become their own.

Journalists, like scholars, write within a
climate of ideas, ideas that fly from newspaper
to newspaper like migrating birds. The hardworking and curious reporter explores each new
idea and collects everything on the landscape.
But embedded in these good habits are dangers,
for both the unprincipled and the undisciplined.

While a virtuous reporter can always avoid
crude plagiarism, crude abuses may be nurtured
by the ethically ambiguous practices that go on
each day in newsrooms. Although I have probably practiced some of these myself, the following procedures now seem dangerous and
unprofessional:

Robbing the morgue. We file old newspaper
stories in the morgue, a misnomer, because some
of the stories live forever. It is a common and
responsible newspaper practice to dig in those
files for background, a sense of history and
perspective. When we cover the trial of a
murderer, we consult the clips on his arrest.

Most journalists recognize the dangers. Do
we, under deadline, borrow paragraphs verbatim
without verification or attribution? Do we recy-
cle old quotations without letting readers know
that a quote may be out of date or secondhand?

Ed Sears describes a case in Atlanta where
"a reporter had lifted some paragraphs verbatim
from the clips. We discovered it only because the
facts he lifted turned out to be wrong, even
though it had been written by a good reporter.
I don't know how much of that goes on. As for
our guidelines, there are none."

Some editors argue that a reporter may borrow an aptly worded paragraph, perhaps more,
from an old story from his own newspaper.

A newspaper may have a good reason for permitting reporters to use information from the
clips verbatim. Perhaps the paper has reduced
a difficult concept (the Consumer Price Index) to

a clear formula, or prefers to use the same paragraph of background for a running story.

In most cases, the writer should assimilate information from the clips and rewrite or let the narrative suggest that material derives from earlier accounts.

Such care becomes essential in an age when technology makes the mining of the clips easier—kidnapping by computer. The *New York Times,* for example, now has a split-screen capability on terminals, which can display a new story on the left and a story retrieved from the clips on the right. "Retrieved information," said a recent story in *presstime,* "can be inserted electronically into the working story."

Abusing the wires. Editors tell of wire stories that appear, almost word for word, under the bylines of local writers. The reverse can happen when reporters from the AP or UPI do not rephrase and summarize adequately the stories of local reporters.

Many newspaper stories combine original reporting with information compiled from news services. Such collaboration has a long history and is essential to daily journalism. But it can be done in unscrupulous ways.

Editors can help create a sense of source for the reader by clearly labeling when wire copy has been used in a staff story. This can be done with a tag line or in the text.

The AP bylaws give the wire service the right to use "spot" news stories from member newspapers as opposed to "enterprise" pieces. According to Louis D. Boccardi, AP vice president and executive editor, AP writers are expected to rewrite stories, although it is accepted that direct quotations will reappear word for word.

"I learned to rewrite everything," says Melvin Mencher, professor at the Columbia Graduate School of Journalism, and a former United Press staffer. "We were told to rewrite and I took that seriously. It had some moral compulsion. But we live in a different age, the age as media star. It's me, me, me the writer. Attribution comes awfully hard to that mind-set."

Lifting from other newspapers and magazines. Broadcast media—from local radio to network television magazine shows—steal from newspapers without attribution in order to preserve the myth of exclusivity.

But newspapers cannot complain. They feast on each other like sharks, a banquet that has gone on for years. Donald Murray, professor of English at the University of New Hampshire and newspaper writing coach, remembers his days as a rewrite man for the *Boston Herald* in the early 1950s. Every day he was tossed clips from all the competing newspapers in town. "It was nothing to turn out 50 quick run-throughs," he says. "Whatever scholarly ideas I had about plagiarism went by the board."

His experience on the police beat also tempered his idealism. "The copy desk would put into my story details from competing editions that I knew weren't true," Murray recalls. "One reporter in town would always find pink panties at a crime scene, even when the cops couldn't. The desk would always put the damn panties in my story."

Even today reporters loot and pillage other newspapers and magazines, using quotations and information without attribution or verification. "A badly trained reporter develops instincts and reactions that are immoral and dangerous for his career," says Mencher. "He's at a small paper somewhere. They're understaffed. He has to write about Sugar Ray Leonard. So he steals from *Sports Illustrated.*"

Looting press releases. When I was film critic for the *St. Petersburg Times,* I received for each new film a press packet of canned feature stories with quotes from actors and directors. It was an open invitation to plagiarism.

Each day, newspapers receive dozens of releases. Responsible editors permit staff writers to work these over, to elaborate on them and check them for accuracy.

A different type of journalism was practiced last year at the *Trenton Times,* where a reporter was fired his first day on the job. "His offense," according to the *Wall Street Journal,* "was not writing up a news announcement exactly as a company had submitted it." The editors had ordered the press release run without a change to protect a big advertiser. The competing paper, the *Trentonian,* published the release without alteration.

"Apparently it's all right to plagiarize from press releases," says Don Murray. "You see university press releases published everywhere, word for word."

Perhaps newspapers should add a tag line to stories taken exclusively from press releases. It could read "released from...." If an editor is ashamed to do that, he or she should make sure the story contains additional reporting, verification and rewording.

Hiding collaboration in the closet. When a number of writers collaborate on a project, care should be taken to preserve the integrity of the byline. Did the person named write most of the story? Are the contributions of others noted at the bottom?

Billie Bledsoe, food editor of the *San Antonio Express,* recently exposed a case of veiled collaboration involving the famous food critic James Beard, whose work is distributed by Universal Press Syndicate. Bledsoe wrote that Beard "has admitted falsifying a column about two meals he claimed to have eaten in San Antonio on September 20." The column fooled the reader into thinking that Beard had attended the events. Beard admitted to Bledsoe that he based his review on notes by an assistant.

Professor Murray says some of his college students get hired as stringers, perhaps to cover local basketball games. According to Murray, the work of his students sometimes appears under the bylines of staff writers.

Cribbing from the books, scholarship and research of others. Reporters have the same responsibility as scholars to attribute work derived from the research of others. The difference is that journalists have not inherited the attributive scaffolding that hangs, sometimes clumsily, on the work of scholars. Nor do they want readers distracted by *ibids* or lengthy parentheses.

Good advice comes from William Rivers and Shelley Smolkin in their book *Free - Lancers and Staff Writers:* "It is unnecessary, of course, for the writer to try to trace down the origins of every captivating phrase.... It is not at all absurd, however, to give credit for a sentence. One worth using should be clothed in quotation marks and attributed to its author. Not...with the footnoting that is common in scholarly journals—but with a smooth note in the text."

Design consultant and journalism professor Mario Garcia is the author of *Contemporary Newspaper Design.* He has seen his work used time and again without proper credit. "When editors do a graphics stylebook for in-house consumption," says Garcia, "they will take huge sections of my book without any mention of my name. That hurts."

The Archdeacon case falls in the category of unattributed research. He could have probably spared himself much grief by simply dropping Jerry Bledsoe's name into the text.

Recycling your old stories. A low-grade ethical problem is the borrowing by a writer of his own work. Even Ann Landers has been caught and criticized for passing off old work as new. As writers move from newspaper to newspaper, they take files of their stories with them and are not above copying themselves when pressed. Such exhumation should be done with the permission of the newspaper in which the story first appeared and with a note of explanation to the reader.

These questions are not designed to put obstacles in the writer's path or to confuse minor abuses with major ones. But misdemeanors can lead to felonies, and an ethically loose atmosphere fosters sloppy work and journalistic malpractice.

While much confusion tangles the issue of plagiarism, some possible paths can be cut through the thicket.

Journalism textbooks and newspaper stylebooks should take up the issue and suggest guidelines for writers. Plagiarism, including the abuses of faculty members, such as ghostwriting of textbooks and kidnapping by professors of the work of graduate assistants, should be discussed in college classrooms. Students should be told—and in writing—what is expected of them.

If I were a city editor, I would call my staff together to talk about plagiarism in all its manifestations and to spell out these reasons for tightening standards:

1) Plagiarism is a form of deception.

2) Plagiarism is a violation of language. Linguists, like Noam Chomsky, emphasize the essential creativity of all language. Almost every sentence is unique. If you don't believe that, apply this test: Count all the sentences in all the stories in the *New York Times* for any given year. How many are identical? Plagiarism is a crime against the nature of language.

3) Plagiarism is a substitute for reporting. A reporter who assumes the accuracy of information in the clips or in wire stories or in textbooks is living in Cloud Cuckoo Land. Of course, reporters consider the source of information and are always fighting the clock. But to the extent that they depend upon the work and words of others, they distance themselves from events and people and create an environment for inaccuracy.

Important mistakes, especially when they turn up in usually reliable sources of information, become fossilized in the clips. "What you get," says Mel Mencher, "is this installation of inaccuracy in the record."

4) Plagiarism is a substitute for thinking. "Writing is discovery," says Donald Fry, professor of English at the State University of New York, Stony Brook. "Plagiarism is second-hand thinking."

5) Plagiarism poisons the relationship between writer and reader. "What readers want to believe," says Fry, "is that they're listening to a real voice conveying his own thought."

Because plagiarism is hard to detect, some editors feel they must fire those who practice it. Gene Patterson fired his offending artist "to send a clear message to the staff."

Other editors have taken milder measures, hoping to rehabilitate the writer, permitting him to work his way back to respectability. This has happened, by all accounts, in Charlotte and Louisville.

There is no agreement on how journalism students should be punished. Some universities view expulsion as the only way to raise standards. Expulsion is what happened to a student at Columbia who "borrowed copiously" from *Newsweek* in his master's thesis.

Others favor less severe punishment. "Plagiarism can be an opportunity to teach," says Neale Copple, dean of journalism at the University of Nebraska. "You make sure the kid never does it again. You don't brand him for life. You just make it a learning experience for everybody."

Free-lance scoundrels can ply their trade through plagiarism. Newspaper and magazine editors who often do not know personally the free-lance writers they deal with should watch out for plagiarists. Free-lancers can more easily escape detection and punishment than staff writers. When a malefactor is exposed, his name should be circulated privately or through trade journals.

This was done in *Liaison* magazine, a journal for evangelical religious publishers. Last summer the journal printed a notice exposing a writer who was selling plagiarized articles, written under different names, to several religious publications. The notice in *Liaison* saved *Perspective* magazine from publishing a plagiarized article submitted by that writer. *Liaison* promised to "spread the word on the cheaters in the trade."

Tom Archdeacon admits that his plagiarism of Jerry Bledsoe was a failure of technique. He failed to distinguish in his notes between his own words and the words of another. If bad work habits lead the writer astray, he is as responsible for the result of his actions as the drunk driver.

Careful work habits help the writer walk a straight line. Don Murray suggests that the first draft be written without notes. "I teach my students not to be a secretary to their notes," he says. "Let it flow. Put all those notes aside. You can always go back to them."

Jacques Barzun and Henry F. Graff, in *The Modern Researcher*, suggest that all researchers rewrite material into their notes rather than copy them verbatim. This practice has three beneficial effects: "You have made an effort of thought which has imprinted the information on your mind; you have practiced the art of writing by making a paraphrase; and you have at the same time taken a step toward your first draft, for here and now these are *your* words, not a piece of plagiarism...."

In the most serious cases, plagiarism is a human problem rather than a technical one. It is practiced by people under duress, people who act without grace under pressure. Editors need to be sensitive to those pressures.

Surely the saddest case was that of Emily Ann Fisher, a reporter/intern at the *Washington Post* who was a Phi Beta Kappa graduate of Harvard. In July of 1973, she inserted dialogue from

Catcher in the Rye into a feature story she had written for the *Post*. She was fired. Friends say she was a brilliant, deeply troubled woman who had a photographic memory. No one is sure how intentional her act was or what emotional pressures led her to borrow from Salinger. But she later took her life.

Ultimately, it is the plagiarist who suffers most from plagiarism. This self-inflicted pain was well expressed by a veteran reporter from the *St. Petersburg Times*, who in July of 1979 kidnapped about one-third of a magazine article on credit cards from *Changing Times*. On the day of her resignation, she pinned a brave letter to the newsroom bulletin board: "Twelve years of dedicated journalism down the drain because of a stupid mistake," she wrote. "I am writing this public explanation for a selfish reason. It will be easier for me to live with myself knowing that the truth is known. But I hope my mistake will serve as a lesson to others. I have let the *Times* down. I have let myself down. But most of all, I have let the profession down. And for that I am truly sorry."